WOMEN IN THE ACCOUNTING PROFESSION

By Shari H. Wescott and Robert E. Seiler

WOMEN IN THE ACCOUNTING PROFESSION

By Shari H. Wescott
and Robert E. Seiler

UNIVERSITY OF HOUSTON

68101

ᴧ Markus Wiener Publishing
W New York

For information write to:
Markus Wiener Publishing, Inc.
2901 Broadway, New York, NY 10025

ISBN 0-910129-40-1 cloth
ISBN 0-910129-41-X paper

Library of Congress Card Catalogue
Number 86-40076
Printed in the United States of America

Foreword

Accounting is a conservative profession, made so by the nature of the function it performs, and like most conservative professions, it systematically excluded women until recent years. In the decade of the 1970's a change took place in many of the established professions, and today the public accounting profession, like law and medicine, is generally open to women. There remain areas, however, in which women encounter difficulty obtaining true equality. This book emphasizes these areas, and, while we do not wish to criticize or castigate the profession, many of the women we interviewed felt that a bit of criticism may be justified. Our purpose is to provide a documentation of the historical, sociological, and cultural background of the opening of this profession to women.

We have endeavored to make this book of interest to those who are currently practicing in the profession, those who are currently training for entrance into the profession, and those who have not yet decided but are considering beginning a university program in accounting. We have taken the woman's viewpoint, which seemed appropriate for this subject, but we have made every effort to keep our biases from dominating or from assuming the position of "women's libber." We hope that the book will be of as much interest to men as it will be to women, for they too have had a part to play in this drama, and they are certainly affected by the events that are described.

The authors are educators, with almost forty years of combined experience as professors at the university level. It is in university programs that new entrants into the profession are trained. Thus we have experienced firsthand the opening of the profession to women, and we have been direct participants. Not more than fifteen years ago we saw bright young women, who were trained, enthusiastic, and eager to use that training, rejected by the profession and unable to find a position that utilized their talents. We saw our classes, which contained only one or two women during the early 1970's, change so that today there are equal numbers of women and men registering for accounting classes. And today women are being recruited and hired equally with men by the very best firms in the profession.

The information gathered as a basis for writing this book is based largely upon interviews with hundreds of women, including practitioners, students, and business persons. Many of these interviews were taped, providing a means of maintaining not only accuracy but the flavor and emotions of the interviewee. Men were interviewed also; their views, biases, and perspectives were of interest in our documentation of how the profession opened itself to women. Many of the interviews were of an informal nature, and were undertaken over a fairly long period of time as we began to explore the subject and the feasibility of writing this book.

We want to express our appreciation to all those who gave their time to us in our data gathering efforts. Many of the interviews took as much as half a day, while some were only five or ten minutes long. But without these interviews we could not have completed this book, and we certainly could not have captured the personal experiences and attitudes that are so necessary for this type of reporting.

We also wish to thank the Educational Foundation of the College of Business Administration of the University of Houston for its financial support of this project. The interviews and writing that underlie the preparation of a book such as this are extremely time-consuming, and without the support which was provided we could not have completed these tasks in a timely manner.

The final expression of gratitude is to our students, all of them, who throughout the years have been a source of inspiration and a wellspring of enthusiasm. Without them, and their counterparts throughout the country, this book and the topic it covers would hardly have been possible.

Shari Wescott
Robert Seiler

Table of Contents

A New Career Choice

Today's women have options open to them that their mothers and grandmothers did not. One of these is the option to practice in a recognized profession such as law or medicine, although some of the recognized professions still remain relatively closed, notably the clergy. Nevertheless, today's options for women include a new array of emerging professions, and public accounting is one of these. The scope of the public accounting profession is not as well known as some of the older professions, but its challenges and rewards can compare with any.

Women entered the workforce en masse during World War II, when "Rosie the Riveter" walked into the shipbuilding and aircraft building industries and proved that she could hold her own in a man's world. During the 1950's and the 1960's the growing commitment of women to the world of work produced a series of both legal and social changes. The Title VII portion of the Civil Rights Act which outlawed sex discrimination was a significant turning point. That provision reflected our changing attitudes and brought a shift in the employment policies of companies in both the profit and nonprofit segments of our society. There were many heroines during this period, and many of their personal profiles and work histories in the public accounting profession will be described.

Misconceptions about Accounting

Public accounting is not a well publicized nor a commonly understood profession, although there are more than a quarter of a million CPA's in the United States. When accounting is mentioned, most people conjure up visions of green eyeshades, gartered sleeves, and small shriveled persons sitting on high stools hunched over dusty ledgers, quill pen in hand. Nothing could be further from the truth. Such misconceptions spring from vivid mental pictures formed from childhood reading of writings such as Dickens' *A Christmas Carol,* where Cratchet slaved as a bookkeeper for Scrooge, and from portrayals in television and movies, in which the accountant is almost always cast as an extremely lackluster character. One of the best-kept secrets of Hollywood is that Bob Newhart, star of movies and television, started as a Certified Public Accountant. His talents as an actor brought more money and fame, so he left public accounting—but there are many in the profession who like to think his personality reflects that of public accountants in general.

The rather adverse publicity has caused the public eye to associate the accounting profession in general with humorless, introverted persons whom Elbert Hubbard, an early twentieth century philosopher, described at the turn of the century as follows:

> The typical auditor is a man past middle age, spare, wrinkled, intelligent, cold, passive, non-committal, with eyes like a codfish, polite in contact, but at the same time unresponsive, cold; calm and damnably composed as a concrete post or a plaster-of-paris cast; a human petrification with a heart of feldspar and without charm of the friendly germ, minus bowels, passion, or a sense of humor. Happily, they never reproduce and all of them finally go to Hell.

True a century ago? Doubtful, but how far from the truth today? Consider the work of Faith Goodland, a manager with the firm of Ernst and Whinney, CPA's, in their Los

Angeles office. As reported in the firm's internal newsletter, *E.W. People*,[1] she administered the day-to-day operations of the complete information system at the Olympic games headquarters. This headquarters facility contained the "command center" for the 1984 Olympic games in Los Angeles, where computerized registration of the 10,000 athletes took place, and the results and statistics from twenty-six different competitive locations were processed and distributed to the 8,000 media representatives who were waiting on the spot. To accomplish this meant the designing of 7,000 computer terminal formats, months of planning and testing the communications network, and training staff and volunteers to operate the equipment. This task is representative of the work done in public accounting today and for the last twenty-five years, and the description given earlier of a wrinkled, sexless robot is as out-of-date as are quill pen and ink. Further, it is of no small consequence that time has changed things so much that the manager in charge of the administrative aspects of this 1984 Olympic project was a woman, not a man!

Perhaps the Olympic games themselves are unusual and made interesting reading, which may lead one to think that what Faith Goodland did there was not just a typical day's task. But it was not an unusual assignment at all. The structuring of complex information systems and insuring that the system works properly are the daily bread of modern CPA's. And they receive very good bread in return for this skill. Managers such as Faith earn some $50,000 to $100,000 annually for their expertise.

The general public misconception may be a holdover from a century ago, when bookkeepers performed tasks that may have fostered personality traits similar to those in the turn-of-the-century description. Grace Hinds, one of the early pioneer accountants, located and reported these business service ads from some early newspapers and described them in one of her publications:

> 1851 Practical bookkeeper and accountant. Opposite the courthouse. Books opened, closed,

posted. Bills and accounts made out. Bookkeeping in all its varied branches taught individually or in classes.

1899　Books correctly balanced regardless of size or number of months or years since last trial balance was made. Experience on 500 ledgers. Average speed posting 70 items per hour. $4.00 per day.[2]

Things have changed considerably in the years since these local newspaper ads appeared. The work of a contemporary public accountant differs from the work done by a bookkeeper as much as the work of an attorney differs from that of a notary public, or the work of a physician from that of a midwife. Bookkeepers record information into the accounting records, while public accountants assist in the planning and decision-making of financial executives, develop information systems that guide large complex organizations, and provide tax planning and guidance to corporations and individuals as well as to estates, trusts, and foundations. The relatively recent opening of this new and exciting profession to women is the theme of this book.

An Overview of the Profession

In 1940 there were only a few women accountants in the U.S., and only a handful of these were certified. Most were doing routine accounting tasks. By 1960 there were 82,000, and by 1980 the number of women accountants had grown to almost 400,000.[3] This rate of growth continues today, and close to half of the 60,000 annual university graduates who receive degrees in accounting are women. While many of these women accounting graduates do not enter the public accounting profession, an increasing proportion does.

The practice of public accounting is not generally understood, and it is nothing like the conception which most people have of accounting work. Public accounting consists of three basic functions: auditing, tax advice and planning, and management consulting. On an audit, the public accountant goes to the client's business, observes the physical processes performed there, examines the records that have been kept of these physical processes, and expresses an opinion concerning the accuracy and adequacy of the company's financial statements. In the tax area the public accountant provides guidance and advice on tax matters and helps the client arrange his or her affairs so that future taxes will be minimized. As a management consultant, he or she may help the client set up computerized systems to capture information which can provide control over the company's operations.

The public accounting profession today is as people-oriented as it is number-oriented. Constant contact with a diverse group of clients in their work environments provides varied and interesting work assignments. There is little wonder that accounting is listed in every issue of *The Occupational Outlook Handbook* as one of the most promising career choices for those who have a facility with numbers but who like to work with people, too.

Carol Subosits, writing in a 1981 professional publication of the Pennsylvania State Society of Certified Public Accountants, gave the following description of her career growth: "Today, I can pleasantly enjoy the perspective of a Monday morning quarterback, since close to six years have elapsed since my first step on the 'audit trail.' Shortly after I entered the profession, I came to know the very diverse atmosphere which public accounting offered. As a female staff accountant I was 'indiscriminately' given the 'opportunity' to tour coal mines, take midnight inventories at aluminum mills, chase fork lifts at a steel mill, climb silos and chemical tanks, and test-count explosives. Like most staff members in a large accounting office, I have traveled extensively and have worked with large public companies as well as many smaller clients. Along with my male counterparts, I progressed to being the senior accountant for a large multilocational client with more significant technical, supervisory and administrative responsibilities."[4]

The Entrance of Women

There are an estimated 250,000 CPA's in the U.S. today, and tens of thousands of persons take the CPA exam each year. However, as with most professions, women are in the minority, and women currently comprise a relatively small percentage of the total. However, today women make up approximately 30 to 40 percent of those who receive the CPA certificate each year, and the proportion of women in the profession is increasing rapidly. Over 40 percent of today's university graduates in accounting are women, and women are being hired by national, regional, and local CPA firms in almost the same proportion as men. But there are some eighty years of male dominance to offset before the number of women equals the number of men. Another ten to fifteen years may pass before this happens, and perhaps even twenty-five may be necessary. But current events indicate that it will eventually happen.

The profession today is generally open to women, and occasional small salary differentials between men and women still exist, but these differentials do not appear to be any different from those existing in the other recognized professions. Starting salaries are for all practical purposes equal, and the salary differences that do exist are mostly at the top management levels. Salary differentials are almost impossible to tie down, especially since partners in large national CPA firms earn from $100,000 to $500,000 annually, depending upon their experience and the nature of their clientele. The earnings of CPA's with local and regional firms are slightly less, and the spread between the top and bottom is greater. Although discrimination has not been totally eliminated, it is lessening steadily. In most firms men and women at entry and mid-management levels receive reasonably equal treatment in job assignments and in promotions.

Women in public accounting face the same general work problems encountered by women in other professions or vocations. There is no magic panacea for the problems of balancing career and family, of fitting children into a busy schedule, and of gaining acceptance as a qualified professional and an individual instead of as a sexual female. However, the nature of the profession does create situations where there is more stress for women than men, such as the requirement of long overtime hours during a crisis period with a client. Long hours may aggravate the problems of caring for children or meshing schedules with a husband. Flexible schedules, on the other hand, may tend to reduce both stress and family problems. One of the purposes of this book is to describe these unique problem areas which exist in public accounting.

As more and more women choose professional fields, such as law, medicine, and public accounting, the belief—strongly held not too long ago—that women in general do not really want professional and managerial careers, or that they are not competent to hold them, must continue to decline. The increasing representation of women in the professions is evidence that women do indeed want and deserve their share of the recognition given to professionals, and they are willing to work and to assume the responsibility required of those in the professional ranks.

A Historic Perspective

This book should be considered a description of a historical event rather than a discussion of women's fight for equality or justice within a profession. Opening the profession to women is a sociological event that is interesting and unique, and is affecting a very large segment of our society. Madie Ivy, a partner in the New York practice office of Peat, Marwick, Mitchell & Company, one of the largest CPA firms, was one of the pioneer women to become a partner in a large international firm. During our interview with her, she focused on the need for a historical perspective in this way: "A description of how the profession opened to women must be treated as history. Those who enter the profession today cannot possibly understand what we went through just fifteen years ago. What today's young women perceive and what goes on around them in their work world will not bear even the slightest resemblance to the problems which I faced back then."

Women who enter the profession today need to know about these early pioneers and their experiences, since we understand better where we are when we know where we have been. The acceptance of women into the public accounting profession is the story of their breaking the barriers of one of the more conservative professions, and the event tended to produce a general broadening of the profession's responsiveness to society's needs. Subtle but profound changes have occurred in the profession itself. Attitudes toward employees in general as well as toward the community have softened within the profession as it has become more people-oriented and more marketing-oriented. How much of this is cause and how much is the result of crumbling barriers to women is impossible to measure, but there was a simultaneous occurrence—and that cannot be denied.

This book spans many decades of change within the profession. Data were gathered from hundreds of interviews, both formal and informal, with women and men who participated in that change process. Educators, students, and business leaders were also interviewed. Public accountants working in both large and small cities in various parts of the nation were included in our study, as were individuals at all organizational levels, from new entering staff to experienced partners. Their experiences, attitudes, and even their biases were captured and are reproduced here as accurately as our recorded interviews permit.

In some cases, especially in the larger international multi-office public accounting firms, we encountered resistance on the part of the male power structure when we contacted women public accountants in their firms. The women in turn sometimes became uneasy about granting taped interviews without formal clearance. They naturally wanted to avoid any displeasure of their bosses or coworkers if they cooperated in what the male power structure feared might be "another national exposé." This term was used a number of times by men CPA's in expressing apprehension about the objectives of this book.

There is a natural reluctance on the part of any group currently in power to admit that other qualified persons are being excluded, and men in public accounting had a natural reluctance to any study such as this which described the problems of "fitting women into the profession." Once convinced that we would give a fair presentation, we were granted lengthy interviews that were taped for clarity of expression and for accuracy. There was a noticeable desire by our women interviewees to tell their story and share their experiences, their fears, how they perceived their work environment, and how they coped with their work problems. They were willing to share their personal feelings with us, and their openness and frankness were very refreshing. However, the strong loyalty they had for their firms dominated almost every interview.

Early Women Accountants

Women have kept accounts since time began. Public accounting, per se, has a more recent beginning. One of the earliest women accountants in this country is mentioned in the autobiography of Benjamin Franklin. This woman had been educated in Ireland, where a knowledge of accounts was frequently included in the education of females in the eighteenth century. Her husband became Franklin's partner in a Charleston, South Carolina, printing firm. In return for furnishing the equipment, Franklin was to receive a share of the profits. He received remittances at irregular intervals but was never able to obtain a financial statement from his partner. After his partner's death, the widow furnished a clear statement of past transactions, managed the business as Franklin's partner, and regularly sent quarterly statements to him. Eventually, she purchased his interest and established her son in the business. This was related by

Franklin because he wished to recommend that branch of education for all young women as likely to be of more use to them and their children, in case of widowhood, than either music or dancing.[5]

Directories for New York City in 1797, 1798, and 1802 listed a Florence Crowley as an accountant. It seems logical to assume that at least from 1797 to 1802 Florence was in public practice, since she moved her office several times during that time. This is the first record of a woman in public practice, and the next definite record of a woman practicing public accounting appears about one hundred years later in 1898 when Margaret and Viola Waring appeared in the listings of accountants in New York City. However, since initials and some first names do not indicate gender, it is impossible to determine whether certain directory listings were names of men or women.

In 1896 New York became the first state to adopt a public accountancy law, and three years later Christine Ross became the first woman Certified Public Accountant in the United States, receiving New York State certificate number 143. After she passed the CPA examination, her certificate was withheld while officials were deciding whether or not a woman could be certified. The minutes of the New York Board of Regents' meeting on December 21, 1899, stated: "Voted that the full CPA certificate be granted to Christine Ross, who successfully passed the professional examination in June 1898." Miss Ross was born in Nova Scotia. Her studies included mathematics, law, and logic. Her accounting practice began about 1889, and early in the twentieth century she was practicing from offices at 17 Battery Place, New York City.

Growth in Numbers

Although very few women were certified public accountants in the early 1900's, a number of them practiced as accountants without certificates. In reports by the U.S. Department of Labor, Women's Division, the following interesting figures were shown under the heading *Bookkeepers, Accountants and Cashiers:*

Year	Women	% of the Total
1870	893	2.3
1900	74,895	29.1
1920	362,715	48.9
1940	475,685	51.1

The 1950 survey was classified differently, and government documents then indicated a total of 55,660 women "accountants and auditors." Since this classification was self-selected by the employee herself, there is no way of knowing the exact duties the women had.

The first women CPA's received their certificates at the turn of the century, and their numbers slowly grew. From only a dozen in 1910 they grew to tens of thousands in the last quarter of this century. The Depression years of the 1930's slowed the entrance of women into the profession, but the war years of the 1940's spurred a temporary surge. However, as later chapters will demonstrate, it was not until after 1960 that women began to enter the profession in great numbers. Up to that point the growth was steady but very slow. A recent study by Slocum and Buckner included the following data:[6]

NUMBER OF WOMEN CPA'S IN THE U.S.

Year	Women CPA's
1910	13
1933	111
1937	130
1940	150
1942	180
1945	250
1948	300
1950	600
1952	757
1954	900
1960	1,500

Slocum and Buckner gleaned many sources to prepare this table, and many of the figures are estimates made by different people at the time. However, the steady and consistent growth reflects an almost geometric pattern.

Roger Trigg, Professor of Accounting at Columbia College, prepared the following table from data in the *Statistical Abstract of The United States,* 1970 and 1980 issues, to reflect the growth in the number of women in accounting:[7]

	Women in the Labor Force	Women Employed in Accounting	Men Employed in Accounting
1960	21,874,000	82,000	414,000
1970	29,667,000	187,000	426,000
1980	41,283,000	379,000	668,000

These numbers reflect all accounting specialties, including public and private accounting, government accounting, internal auditing, and even some accounting educators. However, the data clearly indicate that the growth rate for women far exceeds that for men.

The number of persons employed in public accounting alone is not available from formal public records, though estimates are possible. The American Institute of Certified Public Accountants, the national organization of public accountants who hold CPA certificates, had a total membership, both female and male, of 220,000 in 1983. Not all CPA's belong to the AICPA, and the total number in the U.S. would be considerably higher, perhaps even double this amount. The State of Texas alone has issued over 80,000 CPA certificates since its first one some sixty years ago. A canvass of all fifty states, Washington, D.C., and all territories would be necessary to accurately determine the number of certificates issued, but then determining the number of holders that were deceased would render the resulting estimate less than 100 percent accurate.

The AICPA does make an annual survey of its members. The statistics it has compiled shed some light on the number of women who enter and who leave public accounting each year. The numbers are less than complete, since the table reflects only the women professionals employed by *member* firms of the AICPA from 1976 through 1983. The four-fold increase during this seven-year period appears to be continuing, although actual numbers are not available at this time. The data presented here were compiled from *The Reports of the Minority Recruitment and Equal Opportunity Committee of the AICPA,* chaired by Ms. Sharon Donahue.[8] As mentioned, these numbers reflect only the women professionals with firms that are associated with the AICPA and cannot be considered a complete census.

Year	Number Hired	Number Terminated	Total Women Professionals
1976	1,563	814	5,783
1977	2,318	1,153	7,209
1978	3,105	1,523	8,514
1979	3,734	1,924	11,070
1980	4,441	2,284	13,294
1981	5,156	3,080	15,984
1982	6,022	3,547	18,509
1983	4,667	3,294	20,850

The data presented in the table reflect the steady growth rate in the number of women hired, and they also reflect the high rate of turnover which is endemic to the profession. Long overtime hours and stressful work create a work environment that produces a high turnover rate for both men and women. However, even in the recession year of 1983, when hiring dropped from the previous year, the number of women professionals working for these AICPA member firms still increased.

Women are now an integral part of the profession. They are needed, and they have proved that they have the abilities to succeed in the profession. Remnants of discrimination exist at various points in the profession, and there is still strong resistance at the top level. The fact, however, cannot be denied that public accounting is now a viable option to young women who are making a career choice.

REFERENCES

1. *E. W. People,* Spring/Summer Issue, Ernst and Whinney, Cleveland, Ohio, 1984, pp. 1–3.
2. Hinds, G., "The Woman Accountant has Come A Long Way," *The Woman CPA,* Vol. 20, December, 1957, pp. 6–10.
3. *Statistical Abstract of the U.S.,* U.S. Government Printing Office, 1980.
4. Subosits, C., "Women in Major CPA Firms—A Reflection," *Pennsylvania CPA Spokesman,* Vol. 2, No. 3, November, 1981, pp. 7–8. (This has been reprinted with permission from the PENNSYLVANIA CPA JOURNAL, a publication of the Pennsylvania Institute of Certified Public Accountants.)
5. *Introducing Women Accountants, Past, Present, and Future,* American Women's Society of CPA's, Chicago, 1958, pp. 4–5.
6. Slocum, E. and Buckner, K., "Women and the Accounting Profession—to 1950," *Proceedings of the 36th Annual Meeting of the AAA,* American Accounting Association, Sarasota, Florida, 1984, pp. 201–203.
7. *The Woman CPA,* Vol. 46, January, 1984, p. 15.
8. Compiled from AICPA reports, 1976 through 1983. These reports are issued by the Committee on Minority Recruitment and Equal Opportunity, chaired by Ms. Sharon L. Donahue, AICPA, New York, 1983.

Duties, Values, and Personalities

All professions have work characteristics that are unique to them, and certain personality traits seem to fit best in certain work environments. Public accounting is no exception. A facility with both numbers and people, a high energy level, and a goal orientation appear to be characteristics that bring success in public accounting.

What Does an Auditor Do?

Over 32 million persons in the U.S. own stock in the 9,000 publicly owned companies existing today in the U.S. The stockholders' primary means of receiving information about the companies that they collectively own is through the financial statements released by these companies. But how can the stockholders be sure that the financial information they receive is correct, or that it has not been altered to hide significant facts? The primary function of the CPA is to audit these financial statements to insure that they are fair presentations of the company's profits and its financial position. The auditor satisfies that essential function through a review of the underlying accounting records that produced the financial statements prior to their release to stockholders.

Early in the economic development of the United States there were many instances in which the managers of a company issued misleading financial statements, causing the company's stock prices on the public stock markets to rise or fall as the result of this incorrect information. These unscrupulous managers would then buy and sell stock for personal profit at these manipulated prices. Since the stockholders indirectly elect the managers and charge them with the financial affairs of the company, there were also many instances when misleading financial reports were issued to obscure poor management. Those who were poor managers were naturally motivated to create financial coverups to protect their jobs.

Such abuses resulted in the need for an independent review of the reports prior to their release to persons outside of the company's management, such as stockholders, bankers, and government agencies. The independent audits that are now required of most publicly owned companies are based upon a complex process of audit steps, extensive data gathering, and a thorough awareness by the auditor of the company's activities, its properties, and its management processes.

The audit report, issued to the owners of the business, is based upon a combination of facts, judgments, estimates, and independently gathered information. The audit process was developed by the accounting profession, which carefully and deliberately hammered out guidelines giving it a considerable degree of uniformity.

Audits start with a careful look at a company's internal control system. The control system consists of all the methods by which properties are protected from theft and misappropriation, and all the safeguards estimated to insure the accuracy with which financial transactions are recorded. A good control system will provide an early detection system for dishonesty. If a company is organized so that those who receive money from sales must turn it over to others for counting, who in turn deposit it in the bank, while still others reconcile bank statements, the probability of mischief is less than if the same person handled all four processes unchecked. An auditor usually travels about observing employees on the job and observing how work is done in order to be sure that internal controls in the company are adequate and are not bypassed.

Auditors spot-check documents, read contracts to be sure they are sound and valid, observe how inventories are counted, and spot-check the counts to be sure they are correct. Conferences are held with management and the company's attorneys to gather pertinent data. Amounts owed to the company and owed by the company to others must be verified. When this long process is concluded, the auditor exercises his or her professional judgment and issues a final opinion about the company in an "audit report." It is hoped that everything checks out O.K., whereupon the report is a "clean" report. If the auditor is not satisfied in all respects, the report will be "qualified," and in extreme cases a "disclaimer" is given to indicate that the auditor cannot express any opinion at all.

Companies pay very sizeable audit fees, and for it they receive a two-paragraph report saying that their financial statements are fair. But they must have this report, because it is required by law for all but the smallest publicly owned companies and because our business community has come to respect this independent appraisal. Without such a report, the company's bankers, insurance companies, and prospective investors would question the accuracy of the financial reports submitted by the managers of the company.

Public accounting as it is currently practiced is of very recent vintage. It began no more than a century ago and became recognized as a profession around the beginning of this century. It was only a few years before the turn of the century that the various states established statutes requiring public accountants to have licenses to practice and to pass examinations before the licenses would be issued. The need for public accountants who would serve as independent auditors grew from the widespread formation of corporations by individuals who did not participate in their companies' management. Audits of the persons who did manage the company was considered sufficiently important that the licensing of the auditors became law.

Income Tax Planning

Besides auditing, two other major services are offered by public accountants—tax advice and management consulting. Many decades ago when income taxes became a significant part of a company's financial affairs, the auditor naturally became the advisor for tax matters. Today income tax activities of many CPA firms exceed their audit activities. Tax specialists are in strong demand and are well paid for their expertise. They do much more than help clients complete tax returns. In fact, completion of individual tax returns is considered the lowest level of tax work, and many CPA's do not engage in this activity unless the return is a very complicated one.

The type of tax work done by public accountants can be illustrated by a recent client engagement completed by a local CPA in a mid-size city. The client was the owner and was preparing to retire and sell the business. The CPA, as part of the work requested of her, was to review the company's tax situation to be sure that all tax liabilities had been taken care of. She discovered that the firm had overlooked tax provisions specifically benefiting this type of enterprise. She recommended a thorough review of inventory costing methods, depreciation schedules, and loss reporting procedures. The result of her reviews produced tax refunds of more than $1 million. This type of tax consulting can hardly be placed in the same category with that done by H & R Block!

Management Consulting Work

As electronic computer systems become the basic method for gathering data, auditors have stepped in as systems advisors for the companies they audit, helping the business improve its efficiency and make maximum use of its resources. This service is usually called management advisory services or sometimes just plain management consulting. Consulting services are regularly and routinely used by corporations, nonprofit institutions, public agencies, and municipal governments.

The following example is typical of a consulting engagement. A company whose rapid growth suddenly projected it into the big leagues unexpectedly found itself with a problem. Should it computerize its operations? The head of the company called in its CPA and asked her what effect data processing would have on the company's profit picture. She prepared detailed cost/benefit analyses, including information showing present costs for manual operations, comparing them to what operating costs would be once the computer system was installed and de-bugged. Her studies factored in hard-to-reckon variables, and she recommended computerization. The company's profit picture has brightened steadily ever since. Even though her fee may have exceeded $35,000 for this advice, the increased profits of the company are greater than that amount by many magnitudes.

Consulting services constitute a sizeable portion of the practice of some CPA's, up to one-third in some cases. The fees paid by clients for this type of advice can be sizeable also, and some consulting engagements may take more than a year for completion. Specialized training in computers, financial reporting requirements, and information systems is frequently necessary for qualification to undertake this activity for clients.

The CPA's audit, tax, and consulting services are offered to publicly owned companies, private companies, hospitals, schools, and even to government agencies. Individually owned companies are regularly audited, even though the financial statements are not released to the general public. A company's bank or insurance company needs the auditor's independent review to support requests for loans or bonding arrangements. There are literally hundreds of thousands of these small, privately owned businesses which call upon auditors for the three basic services they provide.

Becoming Certified

But how does one become a CPA? The CPA certificate represents the competency necessary for entrance into the profession, and the requirements to sit for the exam differ from one state to another, although most states require a university degree and two years of public accounting experience. However, a uniform examination is administered nationally by the AICPA, whose headquarters are in New York City. The exam takes two and one-half days to complete and is given twice annually, in May and November. One-half day of the exam is devoted to theory, another half day to auditing, another half day to law, and one full day to federal income tax and regulations and the solution of complex accounting problems.

The exam is rigorous, and only about one in five persons who take the exam will pass all parts of it. Many persons take it over and over again, and some pass after four or five tries, while others never make the grade. When I took the exam many years ago* there was a man who must have been close to sixty years of age sitting a few tables from me. At the lunch break I asked him if he had taken the exam before. He told me he had been taking it for almost ten years—and that he was going to continue until he was successful! I never saw him again; I hope he made it.

Public accounting firms will normally retain new staff persons from three to five years, waiting for them to pass the exam and receive their certificates. If the staff person has not passed the exam in that period of time, the firm's partners consider that the individual does not have the qualifications to be a successful CPA, and plans for releasing the individual are made.

The written examinations are administered by personnel under the guidance of the various states, but they are graded by experienced and trained graders who are CPA's working for the AICPA in New York City. The AICPA brings together a large battery of these graders and provides training prior to each examination. The graders then receive the exams from the various states and they are "blind graded"; that is, the names are removed so that the grader does not know whose paper is being assessed. The results of the grading process are returned to the separate states, and the state boards notify the candidates whether they passed or failed. Primary responsibility for the examination process and for final grades rests with each state board, but the AICPA is the centralized organization that constructs, pre-tests, and initially grades the exams given in all the separate states. In this way consistency in the examination process is maintained throughout the U.S. and its territories. Candidates receive only the final grade; they do not receive the test papers back nor do they receive any information on weak or incorrect answers.

In approximately forty of the fifty states all CPA's are required to take professional development courses every year to keep their skills up-to-date. These requirements differ, but most states require thirty or forty hours of in-class training within each two-year period. Proof that the individual has satisfied these requirements must be submitted when the CPA renews a license to practice each year with the state board of public accountancy. National organizations of CPA's, state societies of CPA's, universities, and many private training organizations provide courses that satisfy the professional training requirements.

The profession is monitored and individual members are disciplined by the boards of public accounting of each state, which have power to revoke the right to practice should an individual violate the public accountancy laws and the regulations established by that state. In general, the profession is governed and monitored in much the same way as those of attorneys and physicians.

CPA Exam Performance

Comparative data on the success of women as compared to men on the CPA exam are not available, primarily because the AICPA and the state boards of public accountancy which keep such statistics will not release them for public use. However, one study did cover the aptitudes of the candidates themselves. This study was reported in 1967 and covered all the candidates who took the 1965 exam.[1]

Nationwide there were 12,357 candidates that year who sat for the exam. Since this was prior to the years when the profession was open to women, only 439 of these, or less than 4 percent, were women. Both men and women reported B averages in the college grades. However, women had higher SAT (Scholastic Aptitude Test) scores than men. The SAT is a test taken in high school that is an important part of the admission requirements of most universities. The median for the verbal portion was 515 for women and 460 for men, and the median for the mathematics part was 574 for women and 550 for men. Women had higher scores on both parts of the SAT exam!

Another source of women/men comparison is the receipt of awards for the highest grades on the CPA exam. Information on those candidates who make the highest grades is available through the announcement of awards which are given to the top 3 percent. In 1976 women won 25 percent of these awards, and by 1981 this percentage had grown to 36 percent. Since this percentage is slightly higher than the proportion of women hired two years earlier (two years of experience is the usual state requirement to sit for the exam), the logical conclusion is that women are doing very well indeed on the CPA exam.

Job Satisfaction

The CPA's work involves contact with people as much as with numbers. Most people think of the accountant as being totally immersed in numbers all day long. While this may be true for some accounting clerks working in non-public accounting jobs, the CPA needs to be as people-oriented as an attorney, and even more so than a physician. The AICPA in one of its recruiting brochures for university students states, "You will be working with people and with numbers almost equally; thus you must be comfortable with both, since skill in one area alone is not enough. Put the two together, add an inquisitive mind, and you are at the starting point for a career as a CPA."[2]

What type of person would be happy as a CPA? Studies have shown that women, in equal proportions with men, enjoy the diverse and evolving problems associated with public accounting work. Both cherish the interpersonal relationships and the achievement rewards which come from daily client contact. In a survey of over 350 women CPAs, the factors which produced actual job satisfaction were:[3]

1. Opportunities to give assistance to others
2. Opportunity for independent action and thought
3. Feeling of self-respect
4. Feeling of worthwhile accomplishment
5. Feeling of security
6. Feeling of self-fulfillment
7. Prestige outside the firm
8. Opportunity for personal growth and development.

These eight dimensions of satisfaction are listed in the order of importance to the women CPAs, with the most satisfying being listed first. The selection of these dimensions as the most significant indicates without doubt that opportunities to help others at the same time that personal growth can take place is the basis of the satisfaction that women CPAs attain from their work. There is nothing strange nor particularly unusual about this list of satisfaction dimensions—women attorneys or women physicians would probably have selected much the same ones. But the results of this study do indicate that the work done by women in public accounting provides the ingredients for a very satisfying career.

Aptitudes

As with all professions and all avocations, certain personal characteristics are necessary for success in public accounting. In general accountants should have the following aptitudes:

1. Intellectual curiosity
2. An ability to work with numbers
3. Orderliness
4. Analytical ability
5. Verbal ability to explain complex matters
6. Goal orientation—ability to see a job through to its completion.

This list of characteristics was not derived as a result of a scientific study, but rather as a result of the authors' experiences and knowledge of the profession. It would in all likelihood be in agreement with such a list prepared by any experienced public accountant. Martin Rosenberg in his book *Opportunities in Accounting* has presented his list of attributes which accountants should possess, and it does not differ greatly from ours.[4]

Do women have an edge over men in these aptitudes? Perhaps so, according to the experiences of one scientific research lab. The Human Engineering Laboratory-Johnson O'Connor Research Foundation, a nonprofit foundation with twelve testing labs scattered across the country, has studied the aptitudes of men and women for decades. They utilized a thorough battery of psychological tests and measured twenty-one aptitudes of men and women. They found no differences between the sexes in thirteen of these, including analytical reasoning, inductive reasoning, number memory, and rhythm memory.[5] They found that women excelled consistently in six others, while men excelled in two. Men excelled in Grip (a measure of physical energy) and in Structural Visualization (rapid assembly of three-dimensional puzzles—central to the technical/scientific professions). The six dimensions in which women excelled were:

* Finger Dexterity—handling, demonstrating, assembling with the hands.
* Graphoria—clerical speed and efficiency, including statistics and actuarial work.
* Ideaphoria—rate of idea flow as used in persuasion and verbal fluency.
* Observation—ability to perceive small changes, alterations in physical details.

* Silograms—ability to form associations between known and unknown words, a measure of memory.
* Abstract Visualization—ability to infer from an absence of structure (This is the complement to Structural Visualization in which men excelled.)

Jon Durkin, the author of the report from the Human Engineering Lab, was careful to point out that no profession or field is the exclusive domain of either gender because of a greater abundance of aptitudes. However, Durkin did go on to say that the aptitudes which underlie successful management are Objective Personality, Abstract Visualization, and high English Vocabulary. Equal numbers of men and women possess Objective Personality and high Vocabulary, but more women reported greater Abstract Visualization than did men. The ratios of high aptitudes for Abstract Visualization are three women in four, but only one man in two. Theoretically, at least, there ought to be more women in management than men. In reality, this is not the case because women have been encouraged by society, both overtly and covertly, to seek and to be satisfied with lesser positions.

As far as accounting goes, the greater aptitudes which women have in Graphoria, Ideaphoria, and Observation should give them a considerable edge in the public accounting arena. These characteristics provide a basis for stronger aptitudes for statistics and actuarial work, for persuasion and verbal fluency, and in perceiving small changes and alterations in physical details. In auditing, tax, and management consulting these aptitudes would be the critical ones. The recent successes of women in the public accounting field seem to confirm the findings of the Human Engineering Lab!

The stereotype of the accountant has been placed under scrutiny in a number of scientific and well-documented studies. In every case accountants as a group were found to be entirely different from the early conception described in the first chapter. One of the earliest studies was completed in 1971 and measured sociability, self-control, flexibility, and self-acceptance.[6] Public accounting partners were found to be more outgoing and more "people-oriented" than engineers and physicians, and only slightly less so than outside salesmen. How different these results are from the impressions so often appearing in television or popular novels.

One of the most in-depth personality studies of women accountants was completed in 1982 by Patricia Johnson and Paul Dierks.[7] They measured the personality characteristics of 100 women accountants who were members of the National Association of Accountants and the American Society of Women Accountants, using the widely acclaimed Personality Factor Questionnaire. This questionnaire measures sixteen personality characteristics and has been used extensively so that average scores on these sixteen dimensions are available for American women as a whole. The table below provides a graphic representation of how this group of 100 women accountants measures against the average.

	1	2	3	4	5	6	7	8	9	10	
Reserved						XO					Outgoing
Emotional				XO							Stable
Humble			X		O						Assertive
Serious				X		O					Happy-go-lucky
Expedient				X		O					Conscientious
Shy			X			O					Uninhibited
Self-reliant				X	O						Sensitive
Trusting		X			O						Suspicious
Practical		X				O					Imaginative
Forthright		X				O					Astute
Self-assured			X			O					Apprehensive
Conservative	X					O					Liberal
Group joiner	X					O					Self-sufficient
Undisciplined					X	O					Willpower
Relaxed				X	O						Tense

O = general population of women
X = women accountants

The scale is set on a 10-point basis, word-anchored at each side with words representing opposite poles of a dimension. Reserved and Outgoing on the first line, for example, represent the far extremes of one of the sixteen personality dimensions being measured.

The X's represent the average scores of women accountants, and the O's represent the average of women throughout all economic and social strata. The 5.5 point on the scale, or midway between the 5 point and the 6 point, is the average of all persons tested, male, female, young, old, tall and short. Women in general fall a bit to the right of this midpoint, but not enough to be of significance. There are a few dimensions, however, where women in general fall to the left—indicating that they tend to be more emotional, trusting, and relaxed than are men.

Women accountants fall to the left of the midpoint in every one of the sixteen dimensions, with the possible exception of the first one, Reserved/Outgoing, where they fall almost right on the midpoint. But this study indicates that women who choose accounting are more practical, serious, trusting, forthright, self-assured, self-confident, and conservative than are most women. These are logical differences, since women in public accounting are business persons with attributes normally associated with success in the business world. In addition, women accountants are much more inclined to be group joiners—which again is compatible with their need for professional associations and the tendency for business persons to be involved in social and community projects and activities.

The general conclusion of the researchers who made this study is that "Women accountants are not aloof and nervous beings; on the contrary, they are self-reliant, self-confident, and, if not extremely extroverted, are at least no more introverted than the average woman. Our study results also have led us to make an observation which could be important later: The accounting profession, in the midst of an ever-changing society, may itself be changing. Individuals who exhibit traits different from the classic accountant's stereotype may be entering the profession."

The same personality measurements were used in a 1984 study which utilized graduating accounting seniors at a major university.[8] This study had similar results and concluded that "The results from the sixteen personality factors indicate that both female and male accounting students can be characterized as Intelligent, Assertive, Enthusiastic, Conscientious, Venturesome, Hard to Fool, Practical, Self-sufficient, Controlled, and Tense. Their ACT test scores (for college entrance) were far above average for both women and men, with females excelling in verbal skills and males in quantitative skills."

Personal Values

Do differences in personality characteristics cause women accountants to want different things from their work than do men accountants? Are the rewards expected and desired from professional work in accounting such that women place greater value on the more intrinsic rewards (those generated internally) such as self-fulfillment, or on the more extrinsic rewards (those controlled by others), such as money? This issue is frequently debated by both women and men in many professions. The conclusions are not always consistent, and perhaps personal biases influence one's conclusions in this regard. However, some rather interesting scientific studies have been made in this area.

For example, Kenneth Earnest and James Lampe undertook an extensive study in 1982.[9] Utilizing data gathered from almost 1,000 auditors, ranging from those new to the profession to those with seven years' experience, the attitudinal differences between men and women regarding work rewards were measured. The results indicate that both men and women ranked six *extrinsic* rewards in the same order. The mean scores of both groups were as shown in the following table when the auditors were asked to rank the items on how highly they valued each one. The value scale went from "1" to "7," with "7" being the highest value.

	Women	Men
Adequate leisure time	6.37	6.25
Promotion	6.07	6.09
Salary	5.82	5.77
Bonuses	5.75	5.80
Challenging assignments	5.73	5.91
Peer recognition	5.57	5.49

The results of this study revealed very little difference in the value structure of women as compared to men, at least as far as extrinsic rewards are concerned. None of these differences were considered statistically significant. Both groups ranked leisure time as the most highly valued, probably because of the normally tight demands on the auditor's time. Having to work sixty or seventy hours per week during the busy season, which can run for four or five months in the winter and spring months, is enough to make anyone value leisure time. Both groups placed promotion as the next most highly valued extrinsic reward, coming before salary and bonuses. Auditors are normally well paid, and even beginning auditors are not exactly in low income brackets; promotion may thus be more important than additional salary. Peer recognition fell in last place for both men and women. The profession provides a considerable amount of esteem and recognition—and perhaps that is why this item fell to last place!

There were, however, some differences in the way men and women ranked the *intrinsic* rewards.

	Women	**Men**
Positive feelings about work itself	5.17	5.26
Positive feelings about opportunities and responsibilities for professional interaction	5.29	5.16
Positive feelings from contact with co-workers	5.54	5.45

While these differences between men and women may appear small, these are *average* scores, and small differences in averages can be significant. Both men and women valued contact with co-workers highest, but women placed responsibilities and opportunities for professional interaction as more valuable than feelings about work itself. Men placed these two in reverse order—work itself was more valued than professional interaction. One could speculate that this difference reflects a stronger need in women to prove themselves and a more strongly felt need to be accepted as members of the profession, but the hard evidence to support this contention is not available from this study. However, it is generally recognized that women still have to do just a bit more than their male counterparts to receive the same amount of recognition!

When this group of 1,000 auditors was further subdivided into four groups, based upon their years of experience, some further differences between men and women became evident. Women who had more than four years of experience placed a much higher value on recognition by their superiors than did the men auditors with the same years of experience. This appears to be a direct reflection of the promotion constraints that are placed on women, for at about this point auditors move into the category of manager and begin to set their sights on a partnership position in the firm. Without recognition of their work and their professional qualifications this final promotion to partner becomes less and less possible. Recognition by superiors at this point was valued highly by men also, but not as the *most* valuable extrinsic reward, as it was for women.

Men with long years of experience continued to place an adequate amount of leisure time as their most valued extrinsic reward—for them recognition by superiors could be taken as an obvious and existing condition. Although assignments and pay may be equal for men and women during the first few years of professional life, recognition of work well done may not be so equal! Thus there may be support for the contention that the preference of male partners for male staff becomes more apparent when one approaches the management level.

In another extensive study, the feeling of reduced opportunity for the final advancement to partner was found to be the underlying reason for the slightly higher turnover rate for women public accountants at the four- to six-year-point. The opportunity for advancement was found to be the key to why a person leaves a job, and the authors of that study, which covered several professions, stated that:

Sex of the employee has almost no relation to the quit rate. Steady upward career movement, which must include correlates in income, status complexity, challenge, and responsibility is, or could become, a meaningful goal for a large proportion of employees, women as well as men. Most recognized motivations for work, ranging from a desire for income and prestige to responsibility and autonomy, are better satisfied at upper organizational levels. The data suggest that at least some of the observed occupational and organizational differences in quit rates can be explained by a structural factor rather than by individual characteristics.[10]

How many women need to be told that there are organizational and occupational differences in the treatment of men and women that have an impact on the quit rate? Not many, to be sure! But just what are these organizational and occupational differences? That question may be just a bit more difficult to answer.

A study of Oklahoma CPA's investigated the felt importance of work characteristics and included ten items which were measured on a 1 to 4 scale, with "1" as unimportant and "4" as very important.[11] The results reflect some significant women/men differences. Remember, these numbers reflect how the individuals ranked the *importance* of the item and not how much of it existed in their present jobs.

	Women	Men	Difference
Opportunity for self-fulfillment	3.83	3.45	+ .38
Interesting work	3.72	3.43	+ .29
Management's concern for employees	3.56	3.20	+ .36
Advancement opportunities	3.39	3.55	− .16
Salary	3.11	3.32	− .21
Degree of autonomy	2.94	2.61	+ .33
Amount of overtime	2.83	2.61	+ .22
Degree of job security	2.72	2.52	+ .20
Amount of overnight travel	2.44	2.27	+ .17

This study indicates that men are much more concerned than women with extrinsic factors, such as advancement and salary. Women place greater value on opportunity for self-fulfillment, interesting work, having a satisfactory degree of autonomy, and adequate management concern for employees. The wide disparity between women and men in the importance given to prestige is noteworthy and indicates a deep underlying difference. These data lend support to the supposition that women strive for self-fulfillment and recognition of their place in the profession, whereas men tend to accept these as givens and search for advancement and prestige.

When these same CPA's were asked to rank the same ten items on the basis of how *satisfied* they were with each one, there was a significant different set of answers. It is entirely possible for one of the items to be very important, and be given a high ranking in the prior table, but there is a difference between the importance of an item and its availability. The *satisfaction* with each item was ranked as follows (stated on a 1 to 4 basis):

	Women	Men	Difference
Amount of travel	3.24	3.28	− .04
Degree of job security	3.02	3.10	− .08
Interesting work	2.93	3.19	− .26
Opportunity for self-fulfillment	2.89	2.84	+ .05
Degree of autonomy	2.82	2.79	+ .03
Advancement opportunities	2.69	3.02	− .33
Prestige	2.60	3.00	− .40
Salary	2.47	2.64	− .17
Amount of overtime	2.31	2.66	− .35
Management concern for employees	2.10	2.60	− .50

Women were slightly more satisfied with the opportunity for self-fulfillment and the degree of autonomy, but men were more satisfied with all eight of the other dimensions. Striking differences appeared in the levels of satisfaction with advancement opportunities, prestige, and management concern for employees. Women obviously felt that those dimensions most important to them were not available to them, at least not in sufficient quantities. The authors of the study concluded that, "The profile analysis by sex provides evidence that the public accountant's job role has been designed principally with the needs and wants of men in mind. If the profession is to continue attracting the highly qualified females which it needs so desperately, then more consideration must be paid to the unique needs of women public accountants. The two aspects of the public accountant's job role that employees are most dissatisfied with are Amount of overtime and Management's concern for employees. These two job role attributes are the most promising for management to direct more attention to if they desire to improve the overall job satisfaction of public accountants."

A Composite Picture

In 1983 Dr. Elise Jancura received funding from the American Women's Society of CPA's to undertake a survey of women CPA's in the U.S. The results of her work were published by the AWSCPA later that year, and the data provide a profile of today's women CPA's.[12]

Education—A total of 96 percent of the women had college degrees, and over 23 percent had graduate degrees. The percentage with degrees has risen from 77 percent in 1964.

Age—Almost half, or 48 percent, of the women were twenty-six years or less, and nearly 70 percent were under thirty. They are earning their CPA certificates at a much earlier age than in prior years; over 30 percent were certified before they were twenty-four years old. The recent heavy inflow of women into the profession is evidenced by the fact that 62 percent of them had received their certificates since 1977.

Employment—Over 60 percent of the women work in public accounting firms, either as self-employed owners of their own firms or as partners or staff of larger firms. Some 28 percent are employed in industry, 5 percent in university or college teaching, 5 percent in government, and 2 percent in nonprofit organizations.

Of those in public accounting, 32 percent are with large national firms, 40 percent are with smaller local firms, and 7 percent are with regional firms. A total of 21 percent manage their own firms, while another 60 percent are in management positions in the firm they work for, either as partners, managers, principles, or supervisors.

Marital status—Over 77 percent of the women have been married, although some are now divorced, and 23 percent are single. Their relatively young age obviously has a bearing on this statistic.

Compensation—Salaries are moving up; over 44 percent earned in excess of $30,000 at the time of the survey. In 1981 only 27 percent earned that amount. Again, the relatively young age of the group has an impact on these data, for those with more years of experience earned the higher salaries.

REFERENCES

1. Bruschi, W., "Are Women CPA Candidates Keeping Up With Men CPA Candidates?" *The Woman CPA*, Vol. 29, No. 3, April 1967, pp. 3–4.
2. American Institute of Certified Public Accountants, *Accounting: It Figures In Your Future*, New York, Publication No. 870091.
3. Barcelona, C., LeLievre, C., and LeLievre, T., "The Profession's Underutilized Resource: The Woman CPA," *Journal of Accountancy*, November, 1975, pp. 58–64. Copyright © 1975 C. Barcelona, C. LeLievre, and T. LeLievre.
4. Rosenberg, M., *Opportunities in Accounting*, National Textbook Co., Lincolnwood, Illinois, 1975, pp. 12–13.
5. Barcelona, C., LeLievre, C., and LeLievre, T., Op. Cit.
6. DeCoster, D., and Rohde, J., "Accountant's Stereotype: Real or Imagined, Deserved or Unwarranted," *The Accounting Review*, Vol. 46, October 1971, pp. 651–664.
7. Johnson, P., and Dierks, P., "What are Women Accountants Really Like?" *Management Accounting*, Vol. 63, No. 9, March 1982, pp. 25–46.
8. Dinius, S. and Rogow, R., "A Comparison of Female Accountant Characteristics with Male Accounting

Characteristics," *Proceedings of the Southeastern American Accounting Association Conference,* American Accounting Association, Sarasota, Florida, 1984, pp. 25–26.

9. Earnest, K., and Lampe, J., "Attitudinal Differences Between Male and Female Auditors," *The Woman CPA,* Vol. 44, July, 1982, pp. 13–19.

10. Reprinted from "Influence of Internal Opportunity Structures of Sex of Workers on Turnover Rates" by C. Smith published in *Administrative Science Quarterly,* Vol. 24, No. 3, September 1979, pp. 362–381, by permission of *The Administrative Science Quarterly.* Copyright © 1979 The Administrative Science Quarterly.

11. Knapp, M., and Rolfe, R., "A Profile Analysis of Public Accounting by Sex and Tenure Intention," *Singapore Accountant,* Vol. 16, 1981, pp. 68–73.

12. American Women's Society of CPAs, *A Profile of the Woman CPA; 1983 Statistical Survey,* Chicago, 1983.

The Early Years

Records have always been kept, but accounting as practiced today is of relatively recent origin. Modern accounting can be traced to a book written in 1490 by an Italian mathematician named Pacciolo. His famous book, whose title translates loosely into *All There is to Know About Mathematics and Accounting,* was written just two years before Columbus set foot in the New World. This new accounting method was called "double entry accounting," and from it came a "balance sheet" and "books which balance."

Women often acted as recordkeepers during the centuries between Pacciolo and the present, and the relationship between women and recordkeeping has been a long and an honorable one. The home was closely related to business during those years, since most businesses were small and were operated from the home. The husband and sons operated the business while the wife and daughters took care of the home and the paperwork. Therefore, it is only in relation to the new profession of *public accounting* that we salute the women of today as pioneers.

The First Women

The first record of a woman public accountant (not certified) in the U.S. was Florence Crowley, who was listed in the New York directory from 1797 to 1802. Whether she was actually the first woman public accountant is open to speculation, given the absence of reliable records.

Although women had received a degree of acceptance into general accounting at the time public accounting originated, their acceptance as public accountants was to be deferred to a much later date. While a very few did take the exams and were awarded the CPA designation, they faced a multitude of problems in developing their practices and gaining acceptance. During the first decade of the 1900's the women who became CPA's could be counted on the fingers of both hands.

The most reliable records of women in public accounting are those of the state boards of public accountancy, who issued the licenses to practice. Elliott Slocum and Kathryn Buckner researched the early recipients of CPA certificates, and in a paper presented before the 36th annual meeting of the American Accounting Association in April 1984, they presented the following list:[1]

Year	State	Name
1899	New York	Christine Ross
1900	Pennsylvania	Mary B. Niles
1902	New York	Cola Sanford Peck
1904	Illinois	Carrie B. Snyder
1907	New York	Harriet B. Lowenstein
1907	Colorado	M. Lillie Geijsbeek
1909	New York	Theodora Daub
1909	Maryland	Florence Hooper
1909	Maryland	Elsa Doetsch
1909	New Jersey	Dora G. Rowarth
1910	Louisiana	Estelle Gapdeville
1910	Louisiana	Frances Knoblock
1916	New York	Lillian Anstie
1916	New York	Myrtle Corbett Heywood
1917	Massachusetts	Alice M. Hill
1917	Massachusetts	Gertrude Briggs
1922	New York	Charlotte Osann
1923	New York	Gertrude Cohen
1923	New York	Jennie M. Palen

Though their list went through 1923, they were able to locate a total of only nineteen names. Due to the inadequacy of records as old as this, undoubtedly others were not uncovered in their research—in fact, two additional women were uncovered in the process of preparing this book. (Their stories are told later in this chapter.) But even if a few were mistakenly omitted, the list is incredibly short to cover a span as long as a quarter of a century. Little doubt exists that the profession was not receptive to women during the early years of this century.

The first woman certificate holder, Christine Ross, was born about 1873 in Nova Scotia. No record is available to tell us exactly where she obtained her initial experience in order to qualify for the exam. We do know that she received certificate No. 143 from the State of New York in 1899 about one year after passing the fourth examination, given in June, 1898, and that she received the third highest grade. Her certificate was withheld for some time because she was a woman.

Bookkeeper in its February, 1900, issue carried an editorial column which stated:

> The eleven men who passed the examination got their certificates promptly, but the young woman waited. A few days ago her triumph came, and now she is free to start out as the pioneer in an entirely new field for women.[2]

Business World in its April 1902 issue, published a full page article and interview with Christine Ross under the title "The Only Woman CPA."[3] She is quoted in that interview as saying, "I think women should have equal opportunity with men to earn an independent living in any business they choose to enter." She was a woman who lived her convictions!

Between 1923 and 1933 a greater number of certificates was issued to women. A total of 111 women had attained their certificates when the Great Depression took hold in the early 1930's. Twenty of these were in the State of New

York. Perhaps New York's lion's share can be attributed to New York City, since it was the largest city in the U.S. and the center of commerce. Larger cities have always presented greater opportunities for CPA's, and today the heaviest concentrations are in the more industrialized states.

Resistance to Women

Although the profession was almost entirely male during the 1920's, women in the profession were beginning to be noticed. *The Journal of Accountancy,* which has always been the official organ of the AICPA (and thus the profession), first took public notice of women in 1923. An editorial in that year stated that university accounting programs were graduating a number of women and that they were being employed as bookkeepers and accounting clerks for corporations. The editorial concluded that prospects for women in accounting were not particularly bright but that there were opportunities for them in some private companies.[4] At least the profession had acknowledged that women could perform accounting work; however, the editorial went on to say bluntly that they were not welcome in public accounting—not even long enough to gain sufficient experience to take the CPA examination.

The reasons given in that first editorial contained the same stilted arguments heard even today—that women could not be expected to endure the hard working conditions, such as long hours and heavy travel, that clients would not accept women auditors, and that men and women working together presented "mixed company" problems. The 1923 editorial stated its primary objections to women in the professions this way: "A staff member may be required to go from one end of the country to another, in company with groups of staff members, working at high pressure and under living conditions not suitable for what might be termed postgraduate coeducation." While the victorian ethics and the double standards in effect then may seem almost comical today, they were very real back in those days.

The reasons given in that editorial were backed up in speeches by men with the stature of Henry Rand Hatfield, one of the grand men of the profession. He questioned his fellow accountants about problems to be expected if women were admitted to the profession, and the list that he compiled and reported in his speeches included beliefs that junior staff auditors would not work for a woman audit manager, that wives would not permit their husbands to travel with a woman member of the audit team, and that women would be gullible and easily misled on audits.[5]

Another objection to women stated in that early editorial proved to be harder for women to overcome: "There is the utterly unwarranted objection, raised by some clients, when a woman appears as the representative of the accountant." Client objection to women auditors was to be the single greatest barrier, because it could be used with no justification and with little way of countering it. A *single* narrow-minded client voicing his objection to a woman auditor could at that time drastically reverse any gains which women might have made in a firm.

Such a situation reminds one of the story which has certainly had national circulation. It concerns an old woman, a young girl, a German officer, and a Romanian officer, all in the same compartment of a train as it entered a tunnel. In the darkness the sound of a kiss was heard followed by a resounding slap. When the train emerged into daylight the German officer had a black eye.

> The old woman thought, "Yes, she is a good girl."
> The girl thought, "How strange that he kissed her and not me."
> The German officer thought, "I wonder why she slapped me when he was the one who kissed her."
> The Romanian officer smiled to himself. "Simply by kissing the back of my hand I have been able to strike the German—and with impunity."

A like situation existed in the 1920's and the 1930's for women accountants. A client could object about a woman auditor to the male manager or partner in charge of an audit, and she would be removed from the audit. The client would have delivered his slap at all women auditors with complete impunity.

Women, then as now, knew that these arguments were more rationalizations than real, but the arguments nevertheless prevented women from entering the profession by placing great odds against them. In many cases women could not find positions in order to get the necessary experience to take the certifying exam, and many who had technical accounting training (some with CPA certificates already in hand) had to take jobs as clerks or receptionists with CPA firms in an effort to prove their abilities. In fact, in fairly recent years one woman who was already a CPA took a job as a telephone receptionist with one of the large international firms in order to prove herself, and today she is a partner in that same firm. It's not surprising that the AICPA produced in 1929 a major recruiting document entitled *Accountancy is a Career for Educated Men*.[6] They meant *only* men!

Adapting to Resistance

In view of the difficulties encountered by women in those times, the matter-of-fact account given by Miss Ethel Kingman of Cambridge, Massachusetts, provides an interesting example.[7] She entered the profession some seventy years ago, and her story illustrates the perseverance, patience, and the willingness to accept the subservience required at that time.

> After my graduation from Boston University in 1911, I taught two years in a small country school in Chester, New Hampshire and did some substitute teaching in Somerville grammer schools. In the hope of finding more satisfying work, I attended Simmons College in 1913–14; receiving the degree of Bachelor of Science in Secretarial Studies in 1915.
> I became a secretary to Assistant Dean Henry A. Yeomans of Harvard College, and started evening

courses at the College of Business Administration at Boston University. There I studied under Professor Charles F. Rittenhouse, who was auditor for the Women's Educational and Industrial Union of Boston. Through Professor Rittenhouse, I acquired the position as head bookkeeper of the Union.

I continued my evening studies at Boston University and took the Massachusetts CPA examination, receiving Certificate No. 200, signed by Stanley G. H. Fitch, President, and Charles F. Rittenhouse, Secretary. Both these men had been my teachers, Mr. Fitch in auditing and Mr. Rittenhouse in accounting.

I received more accounting experience in the office of Herbert F. French & Company, where Mr. French himself was the moving spirit and where after his death I continued my work under his son Earle M. French, covering thirty-five years of experience in all.

As Miss Kingman's story indicates, finding someone to open the door was essential in those early days. Even after the certificate was obtained it was extremely difficult to begin practice. One of the only avenues open to women who did not wish to continue in the employment of their benefactor was to open their own office. Those who chose this route were invariably restricted to small business or to women clients. The world was just not ready for women auditors, tax consultants, or financial advisors.

The attraction of women CPAs to small clients was a matter of both choice and necessity. Large staffs are necessary to complete the audit of a large client, and a woman in practice for herself could not expect to maintain a large staff unless there were a number of large audits to keep them busy. Large clients require large public accounting firms to service them, and a woman practitioner in those days rarely had that kind of clientele.

Women at the time rationalized their position, as reflected in a statement by Marian Frye, president of the American Women's Society of CPAs some thirty-five years ago.[8] "We'd rather have small clients to whom we're advisors and friends, than become just specialists in figures. Besides, big accounts sometimes aren't very profitable." At the time of this statement figures were available indicating that the average income of women CPAs was $10,000 annually, an amount some four times greater than the average income of other working women.

Making the Headlines

During the decade of the 1920's, the few existing women CPA's made their presence known, and reference to some of them appeared in various professional journals. As the job of tax specialist was evolving, women were beginning to take their place as tax advisors also. *The National Income Tax Magazine* contains a reference in its March, 1926, issue to one of the first women to achieve success as a tax specialist. A short description and picture of Miss M. E. Welborn appeared in that issue—her first name was never given. The entire description follows:

> Among the few women actively engaged in income tax practice is Miss M. E. Welborn of Dallas, Texas. She also has the distinction of being the first woman to pass the certified public accountancy examination and to obtain a license to practice in the State of Texas.
>
> Miss Welborn was initiated into the mysteries of the income tax while employed in the Treasury Department at Washington, where she served as an auditor in the income tax department and attended school at night in the study of accountancy.
>
> Her record in Washington was so favorable that Judge A. S. Walker, formerly Internal Revenue Collector, who entered private practice after the close of his term, made her a business offer which led to her association with him in tax practice with offices in Dallas. After being licensed as a certified public accountant Miss Welborn entered into professional practice on her own account and has been very successful.[9]

The article prompted a number of responses about other successful women. As a result, the next issue, in April of 1926, carried a picture and a short biography of Miss Florence Sivertson, a second woman who was a successful tax practitioner. Her story was described as follows:

Publication in last month's issue of the accomplishments in the accountancy profession of Miss M. E. Welborn of Dallas, Texas, promises to reveal that there are a number of other women who have attained exceptional success in this field.

Texas has demonstrated its chivalry in the choice of a woman for governor, as has also Wyoming, but there is evidence that in other states it is equally possible for women to take rank in the forefront in occupations generally regarded as open only to men. Illinois, for example, numbers among its most successful accountants and income tax practitioners, Miss Florence L. Sivertson of Chicago.

She has the distinction of being the first woman to qualify for certification under the laws of the State of Illinois, and of being the first woman admitted to membership in the Illinois Society of Certified Public Accountants. The latter organization changed its bylaws to admit her. She is also a member of the American Institute of Accountants.

Miss Sivertson has practiced in the field on her own account since 1912, and is eminent for her enterprise in having built up an increasingly successful and lucrative practice in a field commonly closed to women. Her staff is composed entirely of women.[10]

Evidently the editors of that journal felt that the matter had been adequately covered, for no other references to women were published. But Miss Sivertson was to be heard from again. In 1942, after almost 30 years in practice, she took umbrage at the manner in which the profession was handling the need for women to fill the places of men in the profession during wartime. She fired the following letter to the editors of *Journal of Accountancy* to let her feelings be known. The editor's snide comment at the bottom of her letter is indicative of the general feelings to which she was taking issue.

Editor, The Journal of Accountancy:
DEAR SIR: Ha! I have been sitting atop my own little stile, lo, these many years, wondering what imponderable would eventually widen the professional accounting crack through which some of us have crawled. And here it is—war!—manpower!

I have probably practiced in the field as long, if not longer, than most of my sisters and have yet to feel the pangs of discrimination against skirt labor (maybe I'm not sensitive). For years it has been my good fortune to enjoy the endorsement and assistance of those of my professional brothers whom I have known. Since 1917 I have had innumerable contacts with Internal Revenue Agents and other Treasury Department workers, and the only member of these taxgathering forces to take a bite out of me wore skirts.

Being no atlas, I sell statistics and fun, believing it unnecessary for so concise a science as accounting to be relegated to the Dry-as-Dust bin. My clients, happily for me, are men who have long since left the cub stage, and it is my opinion that the woods are full of them. Since brains are sexless, and since a comprehension of the basic fact that two plus two, considered calmly and dispassionately, can combine only into four, is not necessarily the God-given birthright of the wearer of cuffless pants, now is the time to turn my sisters loose in the woods and prove to ourselves that they can see the forest in spite of the trees and the skirts.

Even in our giddiest moments, do you doubt that we, the humbler and lesser sex, could have made a worse mess of the world than the one in which we now find ourselves? Isn't this argument enough?

Yours truly,
FLORENCE L. SIVERTSON
Chicago, Ill.

(NOTE.—The answer to the question in the next-to-last sentence of this letter is, No, Madam, we do not doubt that you could have.—*Editor.*)[11]

Before the War Years

The early pioneers could hardly afford to be shy and retiring, not in a profession which refused to accept them. Their first chance came during World War II, when they were needed to fill the ranks depleted by men called to service.

The years that led up to World War II were slow for the

entire economy of the U.S., and the Depression of the 1930's prevented any sizeable growth in most sectors of the economy. Women's place in the profession was not enhanced, to say the least, and the rate of growth of women in the profession slowed during that period. The number of women CPA's increased by only 39, from 111 to 150, during that entire decade.

Strides were being made in the recognition of women, however, because the number of women in the profession had reached the "critical mass" level. There was a sufficient number of them to be noticed within the profession and to provide each other with both emotional and professional support. Women within the profession appeared to have an increased desire for recognition, and one of the primary means of achieving recognition was to unite—to organize. And organize they did. By 1940 the American Women's Society of CPA's had sixty-six members, located in twenty different states. The impact of this and its sister organization, the American Society of Women Accountants, was great indeed; a detailed discussion of the formation and growth of these two organizations is given in a later chapter. To this day the two organizations continue to thrive and are well known throughout the business community.

The two organizations formed a coalition, and they began to get publicity as early as the 1930's, although the publicity was not always what they wanted. Gertrude Priester was one of the early organizers of the two groups, and she proudly related the story of an incident which occurred during those early years.[12] During one of their annual meetings, a reporter from a New York newspaper left word at the hotel that he wanted to interview her and the then-president of the ASWA, Ida Broo. Unable to remain for the interview, Ida encouraged Gertrude to keep the appointment. All who knew of the pending interview were excited that the groups were going to get some much deserved publicity. Gertrude arrived at the appointed time and place and, to her amazement, who was there to interview her but the editor of the Woman's Cooking page. He wanted to know what she could cook! Recovering from the shock, Gertrude thought up some "really screwy" recipes on the spur of the moment. When the article with her picture came out in the newspaper, it created somewhat of a stir. There stood the president of the AWSCPA, a professional woman, and the picture they had selected to publish showed her with a coffee pastry practically in her mouth. As a result of this publicity, Gertrude received a number of letters, one from a woman who said she tried the recipes and found them terrible. Another letter was from the President of the New York Society of CPA's, who said he felt the papers would soon be flooded with recipes from women CPA's. Gertrude promptly responded, "Then an epidemic of stomach trouble will follow."

Although the number of women in the ranks of the public accounting profession remained small prior to World War II, the other areas of accounting were beginning to open a bit. Positions in government accounting were the first to open in a manner approaching equality. The civil service framework undoubtedly played a role in making positions available to women in that area. Many women CPA's, unable to practice their expertise in the auditing area, moved into these government positions. The Securities and Exchange Commission, Federal Power Commission, Internal Revenue Service, and similar agencies experienced a surge of activity and needed qualified accountants. The pay was slightly lower than comparable positions in industry, but by the early 1940's women were accepted to staff these openings. At the same time, industry was being required to submit more and more reports, forms, and schedules to the various government agencies, creating a need for additional accountants in industry. Gertrude Priester estimated that there were 180 women CPA's by the end of 1941, the beginning of World War II, and that about half of them had established their own practices and the other half were in industry.[13]

The War Years

It was not until the war years of 1941 through 1945 that the profession of public accounting itself began to feel the crunch of inadequate personnel. Women were somewhat reluctantly utilized during those years to fill the emptied ranks of men. The rationalization of the established male profession is evidenced in this editorial in the 1942 issue of *Journal of Accountancy*.

> Recent writings by prominent women accountants on these points have given these prejudices a slightly "Life with Father" tinge. The rigors of nursing, of factory work, and of other occupations, these writers maintain, prove the fitness of women for the more strenuous areas of the accounting field. Some clients, it is true, may object to women auditors, but it is logical to believe that some types of enterprises might actually prefer them.
>
> Neither of these questions bears, however, on the advisability of engaging women for staff work in the accountant's office. To relieve men for audit work, women accountants might well do such tasks as report reviewing, statistical analysis, and office management. The feminine virtues of patience, perseverance, attention to detail, and accuracy, on top of sound training in accounting, would fit them admirably for such careers.[14]

The acute shortage during these war years even produced overt attempts by public accountants to induce women to join CPA firms. The New York Society of CPA's established a Committee on Wartime Problems, and one of its functions was to reduce client objections to women assisting on the audit, and to attract qualified women to the profession.[15] Interestingly, the job of accomplishing this task was assigned to a subcommittee composed solely of women members!

There is little wonder that the search for qualified women that was undertaken during these war years was not particularly successful. Decades of suppression of women in the profession had produced few with the necessary training and experience to organize and manage a complex audit. The few women university graduates that existed were snapped up quickly, and some firms began to hire women during their senior years of college, not even waiting for them to graduate.[16]

A total of 821 women were employed in public accounting, according to a survey taken in 1943 by the War Manpower Commission. This was an increase from 480 women two years earlier, but still comprised only 9 percent of the total professional staff in those firms. Only 26 of these held CPA certificates, while the remainder were noncertified and performed staff assignments. Less than one-third of them had as much as three years of experience, which is normally not sufficient to assume a leadership role in even a medium-sized audit. The War Manpower Commission study concluded that with a loss of audit personnel to the war effort approaching one-third of the total public accounting profession, the entire supply of available qualified personnel, both men and women, would be only about half enough to fill the then existing needs.

The lack of acceptance of women by the male dominated profession, even in the 1940's when women were needed badly, was reflected by an incident occurring to Lee Ella Costello, who became president of the AWSCPA in 1957–58.[17] She remembers that in the mid-1940's an attorney reminded her that she should not affix "CPA" after her signature. To be able to do so, he said, one had to pass a very, very difficult examination. He was astonished when she replied that she had done just that!

The entrance of a woman into the profession was sufficiently rare to capture the public's attention. Heloise Brown, later to become president of the AWSCPA, made front page headlines in 1942 as the first woman in Houston to pass the CPA exam.[18] She was the fourth in the state, the first being Miss M. E. Welborn in 1926. Heloise Brown was to become a force to be reckoned with in her native state of Texas. The Houston Chapter of CPA's, hanging on to its male image of the profession, would not allow her to attend their meetings during those early war years. But later, after a bit more acceptance of women, she became an official delegate of the male dominated AICPA to the First Inter-American Accounting Conference in San Juan, held in May 1949.

Heloise Brown became interested in an accounting career shortly after she graduated from Baylor College, later to become Mary Hardin-Baylor College, in Belton, Texas. While an employee of the Monarch Furniture Company in Houston, she became fascinated with auditing as a result of her association with an instructor of accounting at Rice University: "I decided that this was an exciting job, and I wanted to become a CPA."[19] And she quickly did so. After receiving the CPA certificate she began work with the Houston based Butcher-Arthur firm, active in the transportation business. Her job required a considerable amount of travel, and she took advantage of that mobility to contact women CPA's in other cities. She also developed an interest in the national women's organizations. She was elected president of the AWSCPA in 1947, and she recalled that at the time there were less than 100 women CPA's in the country. At the age of 32 she was named outstanding business woman in Houston.

Heloise Brown has been an individual practitioner since 1963, and she feels that she has seen a considerable change in the profession during her lifetime. Of her early years, she says, "I think the profession has been extremely good to me, and the doors that were open to me would normally not have been open to a woman." It gave her a national reputation, a busy and productive lifestyle, and considerable monetary rewards. Her mark on the profession continues to be felt in the Southwestern states.

Academic Resistance

During the 1940's colleges and universities were not encouraging women to study for the profession although obviously some, like Heloise Brown, did. Professors of accounting at that point were almost all male and were indoctrinated with the concept that the accounting profession was suitable for men only. Women who appeared in a university accounting class were subtly but effectively counseled about the lack of opportunity, especially in public accounting. Heloise Brown Cantor did receive exceptional counsel in that regard, since she was encouraged by her Rice University instructor friend to become a CPA.

Beta Alpha Psi, the national honorary fraternity with chapters on almost every campus with a strong accounting program, did not accept women as members until well into the 1950's. In 1952 the national charter of Beta Alpha Psi was amended to accept women, but even then all of the individual chapters did not yield to the national mandate.[20] Seven chapters did not change their local practices to conform, and two chapters specifically voted to continue to exclude women. Interestingly enough, today almost every chapter in a coed institution is more than 50 percent women, and the leadership is in many instances more feminine than masculine. But in the 1940's, to admit a woman member was unthinkable.

After the War

Unfortunately the limited gains that women were able to make during the war years were short-lived. Women were accepted only out of necessity, and, when the war ended and men returned, the welcome they had received was no longer offered. Between 1942 and 1945 the number of women CPA's almost doubled, from 150 to 280, but once again these women had to turn to the establishment of their own firms or to positions in industry, since in the post-war years they were once again systematically excluded. Jennie Palen, a woman CPA who went through the war era, wrote in 1945 that women were performing at satisfactory levels, that clients did not object to them as members of the audit team, and men auditors also accepted them as team members.[21] However, what she perceived as acceptance was built upon necessity. By 1953 her opinion changed, and in another article she wrote that men were replacing women and that the barriers were again in place.[22]

The reversal to prewar status came as a result of an oversupply of accountants that occurred in 1948 and 1949 when tens of thousands of war veterans who had returned to college after the end of World War II began to graduate. University programs in accounting during those post-war years were very popular, and a steady stream of men became available to the profession. The strides that women made during the war were indeed short-lived. Marguerite Gibb, a Seattle CPA, said in 1954 that although resistance to women was being experienced, she was optimistic that some progress had been made. She stated her perceptions this way:

> The usual objections to women in professions have unfortunately persisted to some extent, but there is hope! Objection on the grounds of lack of ability has been substantially discounted. Women proved themselves during the war, when many of them did outstanding work, in jobs otherwise held by men. Not only that, they were found by their employers and fellow workers to be congenial, retaining their femininity without using this so-called weapon as a means to secure special treatment.
>
> The old adage that women increase the personnel turnover because they have a tendency to get married and leave their jobs, has proved a misinterpretation of fact. Women do leave their jobs, but so do men. In one firm, a count was taken, and out of four women employed, one remained after four years; but out of twenty men hired, only two remained after six years.
>
> In the long run, it is up to women to see that their progress in the field continues and accelerates. All that women ask of their fellow members in the profession is that they base their qualifications for employment solely on factors of ability and competence, and never let a pretty face dissuade them.[23]

Following World War II a new set of rationalizations was necessary. Women had proved they could perform well in the profession, and the male dominance required a reformulation of the reasons for not including women. These new rationalizations led to beliefs that the profession was not to be blamed if few women or blacks applied. After all, wasn't a profession an outgrowth of natural relationships among like-minded and like-mannered people, and therefore unlike people, such as women and blacks, would naturally shy away? And wasn't the self-selection process within a profession such that unlike-mannered persons would not fit and would terminate anyway? Such rationalizations as these dominated the late 1940's through the 1950's.

Changing Perceptions

The profession's treatment of women changed sometime in the 1960's, in large measure because of a shortage in qualified personnel. But even more significant was the new legislation curbing unequal treatment of women and other minority groups. This legislation reflected an awareness that was not there in prior eras. Men became more aware of the unjust exclusion of women, and women became more aware of the existence of hidden, insidious discrimination. It took a combination of changed management perceptions on the one hand and changed expectations by women on the other to effect changes in the discriminatory practices within the profession. Without altered perceptions on both sides, the changes that did occur would have been much later in coming. And even so, a long period of time was required for the distillation and implementation of these altered perceptions—several decades of time. But the changes which first began during the war years did eventually open the doors.

REFERENCES

1. Slocum, E. and Buckner, K., "Women and the Accounting Profession—to 1950," *Proceedings of the 36th Annual Meeting of the AAA,* American Accounting Association, Sarasota, Florida, 1984, pp. 201–203.
2. *Bookkeeper,* February, 1900, Vol. 12, No. 8, pp. 94.
3. *Business World,* April, 1902, Vol. 22, pp. 175.
4. *Journal of Accountancy,* December, 1923, Vol. 36, pp. 443–444.
5. Quire, C., "Pioneers in Accounting," *The Accounting Review,* Vol. 22, No. 1, January, 1947, pp. 74–79.

6. American Institute of Certified Public Accountants, *Accountancy is a Career for Educated Men,* New York, 1929.

7. *AWSCPA News (Membership letter),* Vol. 12, No. 5, May, 1967.

8. "Women CPA's, 600 in U.S., Make Money, Prefer Small Accounts," *Journal of Accountancy,* Vol. 90, No. 6, December, 1950, pp. A–17.

9. "Texas Woman CPA Succeeds in Tax Practice," *The National Income Tax Magazine,* Vol. 4, No. 3, March, 1926.

10. "Women Who Have Won Distinction in the Profession of Accountancy," *The National Income Tax Magazine,* Vol. 4, No. 4, April, 1926, p. 138.

11. "Women in Accounting," *Journal of Accountancy,* Vol. 74, No. 1, July, 1942, p. 67.

12. American Women's Society of CPAs, *Celebrating Our Past, Present and Future,* Chicago, 1983.

13. Priester, G., *The New York CPA,* Vol. 12, No. 8, May, 1942, pp. 466–469.

14. *Journal of Accountancy,* Vol. 73, No. 4, April, 1942, p. 295.

15. Palen, J., "The Position of Women Accountants in the Post-War Era," *Journal of Accountancy,* Vol. 8, No. 1, July, 1945, pp. 27–30.

16. "Personnel Situation in Public Accounting Firms," *Journal of Accountancy,* Vol. 78, No. 2, August, 1944, pp. 173–175.

17. AWSCPA, op. cit.

18. "Houstonian is Pioneer Woman CPA," *Houston Chronicle,* Sunday, May 4, 1952.

19. Harvison, J., "Women CPA's Come of Age," *Texas Society of CPA's News,* Vol. 1, No. 6, January, 1975, pp. 9–10.

20. Gibb, M., "The Place Women Occupy in the Accounting Profession," *Journal of Accountancy,* Vol. 98, No. 4, October, 1954, pp. 502–503.

21. Palen, J., 1945, op. cit.

22. Palen, J., "Women in Accounting, 1933–53," *Accounting Forum,* Vol. 24, May 1953, pp. 51–54.

23. Gibb, M., 1954, op. cit.

The Barriers Crumble

When men returned to the work force following World War II, the profession for all practical purposes ceased to hire women. Through direct replacement, men assumed the jobs that women held. When the busy season ended during the years of 1947 and 1948, women were not retained on the workforce; and when the next busy season arrived, men were hired in their place. Those women who had CPA certificates could begin their own firms, but many had to move to jobs in industry and government.

The Change Begins

During the 1950's the seeds of change were planted. Large numbers of men were recalled to service for the Korean conflict, at the same time that the economy was booming. Public accounting firms needed greatly increased staffs, more than could be satisfied by the male graduates of university accounting programs. A similar shortage of trained personnel existed in many of the other professions and in most areas within the economy.

The Civil Rights movement during the 1960's also had an impact upon the acceptance of women, and the significance of women in the work force was beginning to be more widely appreciated. Discrimination also became a more recognized phenomenon, and pressures were mounting to alter some of the more discriminatory practices. At this same time passage of Title VII of the Civil Rights Act provided the legal basis for curbing sex discrimination in both work and education. Women's activist groups were more visible, and women began to move in increasing numbers into all the professions.

In 1960 the number of women in public accounting was low indeed, but the number was at least commensurate with the number to be found in other professions. There were 6,600 women engineers in the U.S. at that time, 9,000 women bank officers, and roughly 1,000 women in high civil service positions.[1] The 6,500 women attorneys at that time made up only 2.6 percent of the total in that profession.[2] Of the approximate 1,500 women CPA's, a large portion of them was with industry or government, and only a fraction was in public practice. Government, university teaching, and industrial accounting work were considered more fitting for women accountants up to this time, and, although the exact number of women in public practice is not known, it was undoubtedly very low.

The 1960 census reported that 16.5 percent of all the accountants, both certified and noncertified, were women. Most of these were noncertified, since women had difficulty prior to this time getting the necessary experience to qualify for the examination. By 1970 the number of women accountants had grown to 25 percent of the total, and by 1978 to 30 percent.[3] This rate of growth exceeded that of most of the other professions. Women attorneys, for example, increased from less than 3 percent of the total in 1960 to only 12 percent in 1980.[4]

University Counseling

The first point of discouragement met by women attempting to enter the accounting profession at this point was at the university level. Accounting professors were mostly men with public accounting experience, and they maintained close ties with the profession. They not only failed to encourage women but sometimes actively discouraged them. The story of Maida Barrick is an example of this kind of barrier.[5] She pointed out that her career choice was discouraged by one of her favorite professors, who was then head of the Accounting Department at the University of Minnesota. He counseled her that there were very few opportunities for women in the field at that time.

Another discouraging word, for her, resulted from prejudice, rather than lack of concern. A professor in a graduate course, she states, said categorically at the first session that he wanted neither undergraduates nor women in any of his classes. Maida Barrick, needing the credits, stayed. She was a manager in the firm of Coopers and Lybrand, known then as just Lybrand, when she made these statements. This international firm is one of the largest and most prestigious of the CPA firms, and her position as manager is sufficient testimony to both her abilities and her perseverance in the face of prejudice and lack of concern.

In similar fashion, Barbara Harvey, a manager in the consulting division of Haskins and Sells (now Deloitte, Haskins & Sells), another international CPA firm, reported the advice that she received. "I was a math major in college. I worked for a while with my father, who is a government contractor doing cost accounting, and when I went back to school, I switched majors. I found that the professors who insisted you'd never find a job were more of an obstacle than anything I've encountered outside school."[6]

Public accountants began staffing their audits with women earlier than professors would admit that these opportunities existed. Perhaps this was understandable, for the professors were basing their opinions upon what they had seen in the past. The signs that overt resistance was slipping away were unmistakable by the mid-1960's.

Subtle Discrimination

Discrimination now began to assume a more personal nature—policies had been formulated and communicated in many firms stating flatly that discrimination would no longer be tolerated, but that did not necessarily mean that individuals would be unbiased. Discrimination was now an individual matter, applied against either individual women or women as a group. Now the more subconscious forms of discrimination became the principal barriers to these first women who came on board. Preferential assignments and male/female segregation of work locations and specialty areas were common examples of the type of discrimination practiced at that time.

In many cases the men principals and partners responsible for work assignments and for establishing office arrangements did not recognize that their treatment of males was different from that of females. It was evident in many ways, with the annual firm outing as one example. The women were informed subtly that it was a male affair in which women would probably feel out of place, that their presence might dampen the activities, and that, anyway, there were no facilities there for women! This was tantamount to saying, "You can work for us, but we don't want you to socialize with us."

Men tended to lunch together and either unknowingly or deliberately failed to include the women when the group formed to leave the building. A more telling bit of evidence of the existence of subconscious bias was displayed when the male explained things to a woman associate on a more elementary level than he would to his male associates, or was obvious in giving credit to a woman for an idea when it really was not necessary to do so.

Preferential treatment for males frequently occurred in the performance evaluations that are required in public accounting. Seniors and supervisors must prepare evaluations of the work of staff that they utilize on an audit, and to expect higher performance of a woman in order to receive the same evaluation as a man was not an unusual practice. Kathryn Krause, an experienced public accountant in Georgia, speaking to a group of men CPA's, gave her own personal views on this subject as follows:

> If your style involves profanity, go ahead. Women don't want to be treated any differently from the male

professionals in the firm. Don't try to shelter the women, treat them as professionals. If women decide they can't get ahead in your firm, they will leave and start their own practices just like the men will.[7]

Her views are shared by Dorothy McCoy who, with a local firm in Lincoln, Nebraska, stated her feelings on differential treatment like this:

Most clients accept a woman staff member on equal terms with a man, if she is presented as an equal by the supervisor, but a man-in-charge who feels that the woman is inferior will convey this impression to the client. This creates an awkward situation for everyone on the engagement.

The young woman is usually welcomed into the firm as a qualified staff member and willingly helped through the indoctrination process. She does not become some kind of moat monster when she enters the male fortress of accounting. She is not trying to prove that she is better than the male of the species. Nor is she a feminist crusader who shudders at swear words and wants lace edging on all the desks. She expects to be treated as courteously by the other staff members as they would treat any other woman, but she is also perfectly capable of opening the door for a man who has a portable machine in one hand and a thirty pound briefcase in the other.[8]

Client Acceptance

Clients also had to adjust to women as they began to appear regularly on the audit staff. They had to learn to deal with this new type of auditor. Denise Devine very concisely expressed the clients' reactions to the new women auditors who showed up in their offices. She categorized client reactions during those days as falling into these three categories:

1. The "It's About Time" fantasy
2. The "How Cute" phenomenon
3. The "Let Me Explain" syndrome[9]

She went on to elaborate:

Number one refers to the standard comment, 'It's

about time we get something good to look at on the audit for a change.' Confused, because in this situation a compliment about my work performance would have been more pleasing, the only thing to do was to smile prettily and continue working.

Number two refers to the category of remarks by clients that included, 'How cute, we have a live lady auditor and she even carries a briefcase!' Some how this one made me feel like a mascot for an advertising campaign . . . she walks, she talks, she uses a ten key with speed and accuracy, etc.

Number three was the most unnerving of all. When I approached the client with a routine audit question the client, upon realizing the person entering his office was wearing a skirt, would pull out every ledger, journal, trial balance, and document in sight. After the question had been asked the client would go to some of the books and documents and answer the question. Before I had a chance to say thank you and leave, the client would say, 'Let me try to explain that another way' at which point he would use another set of documents to answer the question again. This would continue until the level of comprehension would befit a ten-year old.

New female staff at that time often felt that they were treated as an oddity. A frequent complaint of the women was that the senior in charge of the audit made excuses for her being there. There is undoubtedly a right and a wrong way to introduce the client to a new woman auditor, and in many cases the introduction was an unknowing put-down to the woman. It was also true that every accounting firm had a few clients who did not prefer and, in isolated cases, would not accept the female. Initial introductions could frequently start things off on the wrong foot, and in such delicate situations client education was essential to acceptance. Failure to "educate" the anti-woman client meant that the supervisors in charge of the audit would have to reassign the woman, and the client-resistance syndrome was further reinforced.

The audit process is itself not something toward which clients look forward. Their daily work routines are disrupted, their office space is cluttered, and there is a fairly high degree of stress associated with having one's work reviewed and errors uncovered and spotlighted. Therefore, clients are not overly thrilled at seeing the auditors come in, whether they be male or female, and the big obstacle to be overcome was the natural reluctance of many clients to accept any new auditor, regardless of sex. Not all women at that time recognized that because of their gender their actions tended to draw extreme reactions. If she was good, she was very, very good; if bad—horrid! With passing years clients became accustomed to women on their audit teams. Clients wanted the audit done efficiently and effectively, and the professional performance of these early women staff members left no doubt about their technical qualifications. By the early 1970's the surprise of clients to the use of women auditors had all but disappeared. They had become accepted by all but the most die-hard anti-women clients. The Ernst and Ernst house organ, appropriately entitled *Ernst and Ernst,* reported on the lack of client surprise in the summer of 1972 as follows:

> 'My God, it *is* a girl!' was all that the foreman of the cement plant could blurt out. A moment earlier, the coveralls-clad figure next to him-clipboard in hand— had climbed to where he was standing atop a tall mountain of crushed stone and said, 'I'm one of the auditors, and I'm here for the inventory observation.' Detecting an unexpected softness in the face, the foreman had lifted the speaker's hard hat, unleashing a cascade of golden curls, and exposing to the sunlight the pretty smile of a woman accountant from E. and E.
>
> The incident was unusual. Not because the accountant was a woman, but because the foreman was surprised to see her in that setting. This was the only instance of its kind (surprise to find a woman auditor) reported in recent interviews with women members of the firm's professional staff around the country.[10]

First Weeks on the Job

During the early days of the 1960's and 1970's, the most difficult period in the career of a woman staff member

tended to be the first few weeks, when she was being indoctrinated to her new job and the people with whom she would
work. It was natural for the new staff to band together to
compare notes as to what they had learned of the firm, the
job, and the personalities involved. The few new females
joining the staff were likely to be excluded from such "bull
sessions" and thus missed out on an important part of the
indoctrination process. Further, all the new staff had to rely
heavily on their senior or supervisor's feedback in order to
know how they were performing. This line of communication, so vital to the progress of new staff, was hampered by
the inexperience of men in working with women, especially
if the supervisors felt that women would likely react emo-
tionally to criticism or suggestions for improvement.

It is almost a truism that the best criticism is offered to
people who take it best. Unfortunately far too many men at
that time tended to feel that women were too emotional in
the face of criticism. A calm, professional attitude during
these stressful sessions was essential, and the stress on the
first women staff was greater than that of men, because
women were on trial in more ways.

The male staff members generally accepted the new
women staff, and problems at that level were minimal. For
the most part they also got along professionally very well
with the female staff. At this level the "natural" relationship
between men and women had not been disturbed. As one
young woman put it, "His masculinity was not challenged as
long as I was assisting him." When the role was reversed,
however, problems often arose. It took more than normal
poise and tact for women to make the transition from junior
to senior staff with administrative responsibilities. Men
often did not want to be criticized, corrected, or evaluated
by a woman.

Problems of Travel

Travel arrangements presented some additional problems
in the early days. Express policies in all firms stated that

there was to be equal treatment, but such policies were not fully effective, nor did they address all the problems that arose. The questions of how much, where, and with whom women staff should travel was one of the more frequently discussed problems of the time. If a woman was sent on the road with the men, her husband, their wives, and any small town gossips might have been upset. If she was kept at home, she may have felt that her professional opportunities and development were hampered by a geographical cage. One frequent solution was to assign the woman to in-office and in-town jobs, unless two women could travel together with the men on the audit team. Our victorian moral structure had not completely disappeared, but two women together eased the minds of those who felt that a single woman traveling with men would tempt fate.

Firms often felt that they were in a position of "damned if you do and damned if you don't" in their attempts to solve the travel dilemma. Males on the staff frowned on any special concessions to women, and their wives frowned on women going out of town with their husbands. Fortunately, the problem fast disappeared as firms realized that the only solution was to count on the maturity and judgment of their staff accountants to handle the situation in a professional manner (and on the male accountants either to gain the trust of, or to pacify their wives). Probably insufficient attention was given during those years to the fact that these new women professionals were not about to jeopardize their newly won positions with indiscreet behavior.

A survey on the subject of travel completed in 1972 indicated considerable unrest as a result of the failure of the firm's management to send women on overnight assignments on an equal basis with men.[11] One woman said that her firm told her that her talents and time were more productive in the office and assigned her detail work there instead of more challenging work out of town. Another indicated that the size of the job and the responsibility she received were less than those assigned to men, which held her back professionally. Several indicated they received more tax work and more office assignments to make up for the fewer assignments they received on out-of-town jobs. This survey went on to gather opinions concerning travel from the women's families, their firms, and the families of males traveling with the female staff. Their summarized results were:

	Full Approval	Limited or No Approval
Female CPA's family	69%	31%
Other members of the firm	65	35
Families of male travel companions	40	60

Note that it is the families, notably wives of the male staff members, who least approved of mixed groups traveling together.

Some travel was necessary, regardless of who approved or disapproved. Travel to professional seminars and training sessions was unavoidable, and some of these programs ran as long as two weeks. A humorous sidelight to women's attending these seminars arose from the difficulty, in those years, of telling women from men by their names alone.[12] In multi-office firms the individual practice offices would send to the executive office their lists of names without specifying which were women. The story is told that an unsuspecting personnel director once made a double room assignment in a New York hotel without realizing that one of the pair was among the new wave of women accountants. It isn't hard to see how such a mistake occurred since the firm had recently hired women named Lynn, Lesly, Merideth, and Dale, along with men named Dale, Terry, Kim, Ronnie, and T. Laverne. To avoid this kind of embarrassing goof the firm now carefully designates women on lists where it is of significance with a "Miss" or "Mrs." after each name.

Feminity—Help or Hindrance?

In business assignments, being a male or a female should be neither an advantage nor a handicap. However, it is a fact that must be accepted (by men and women alike) that both femininity and masculinity can be used to advantage in some situations. Some women use their femininity to advantage occasionally, others frequently, others not at all. In public accounting the general guideline of women during this first wave of feminine accountants was that they had to make other people comfortable with the fact that they were women as well as professionals. The extremes of assuming the helpless female role, or of being ruthlessly determined to outdo every male on the staff, are hardly ever a wise strategy. Those who followed either of these were not likely to be successful in the long run.

In those early days women sometimes took on the manners of their male associates as a defense mechanism. They rejected their own role and attempted to become "one of the boys." While this worked for some, it was a dangerous approach for most. People are generally uncomfortable around someone who acts affected or tries to be something that he or she really is not. Both men and women tend to like women who are women. However, by the 1970's the acceptance of women was such that they were able to bring a new dimension to the profession—a distinctly feminine touch. This "touch" is for men a mysterious combination of warmth, character, and a welcoming countenance. It is the quality of caring for others that lies at the heart of the feminine mystique. When a truly professional woman is associated in business with a group of men, she is aware that she has the opportunity of making this a worthwhile human experience for them and for herself. Gentle assertiveness on the part of a woman tended to be more becoming and more effective. It was in those days, and continues to be so today.

Carol Subosits, while a tax manager with Deloitte, Haskins, and Sells stated that, "I would not be so naive as to say that being a woman has never helped me, in that the social atmosphere of our times looks favorably on women in business. I carefully distinguish this general climate from preferential treatment in that our novelty as professionals often allows us to put a foot in the door, but does not guarantee promotion or success."[13]

Her feelings were shared by Stephanie Shern, a principal

in the New York office of Arthur Young. She was very open about matters of preferential treatment and gave insightful answers to some very pointed questions concerning whether she ever felt she had received preferential treatment from Arthur Young, and whether the firm gave any special help to her because she was a woman.

> I'd have to answer that, most definitely not, it did not give me preferential treatment. It did not, because I am a woman, sit down with me and say, Okay, Stephanie, we want you to be our next woman partner and this is the career path we see for you to get there. I've been told by some of my peers and partners from other public accounting firms that if I were with their firms, that would have been done for me. But at Arthur Young and Co. the partners believe that a woman, a man, a black, an Oriental—anyone and everyone has to perform and to meet the standards that have been set by the partners and must be judged on the objective merits of that performance. I would like to have thought that being a woman would be helpful to me, and I'm not naive enough to say that it has not been, but I would have to say that I have definitely not been given preferential treatment.[14]

When Stephanie Shern was asked whether this was a contradiction—that being a woman has helped her but that she didn't receive preferential treatment, she answered:

> Arthur Young hasn't given me preferential treatment, but the climate of the times is such that socio-business conditions are favorable—and sometimes preferential—to women. I'm glad I'm a woman in a business profession at this time. Of course, my future success will be based on my credentials, technical skills, and competence—and not on the fact that I'm a woman.

When asked whether clients were more receptive to her on engagements because she was a woman, she said:

> I would have to say that, in the ten years I have been with Arthur Young and Co. it's worked both for me and

against me to be a woman. I think it was more of an advantage in my earlier years with Arthur Young than it is now. At the level I am now, when I deal with the men who have responsible positions in client operations, at times they're not really sure of my position, because I'm operating on their level. Yet when I first started, it was very simple for clients to accept the fact that I was there doing the job that I was sent to do, because I was working at a lower level—and the client person was above me. I was no challenge to his or her authority. I was there to get an audit done—but I was not then dealing one-on-one.

Many of the women we interviewed in the preparation of this book expressed the same feelings. Their femininity opened a few doors at the lower levels of their careers, but they found that upon reaching management levels, the advantages of femininity disappeared; in fact, femininity became a disadvantage when a position of heavy client responsibility was reached. At that higher level both clients and subordinates began to question her position, and convincing them of her rightful place there became necessary. Competency, professional skills, and, perhaps more importantly, interpersonal skills became the means by which this persuasion was accomplished. Femininity at higher levels became a liability rather than an asset.

Assuming Client Responsibility

After four or five years, staff accountants reach a level of responsibility that gives them direct and meaningful contact with controllers, treasurers, vice-presidents, and presidents. Their daily work assignments include some tough negotiations with these men who are experts at that endeavor. After the first wave of women had reached the administrative level, evidence clearly indicated that they were scrutinized more closely by the partners in their firm than were men at the same level. It seemed that women who earlier were considered just short of being overbearing were now perceived as too quiet and as not being able to stand toe-to-toe with these tough client executives.

Women who were not aggressive were labeled as unasser-tive; women who earlier felt that they were able to use their femininity as an approachable advantage with clients had to learn new approaches. Sometimes the need for this kind of shift caused the pendulum to swing too far, and a real danger existed of overaggressiveness to the point of being personally distasteful. Finding the right balance of femi-ninity and aggressiveness was not always easy, and women entering the management level of the public accounting firm faced a particularly tough period of adjustment. Males were not as subject to the need, at this point in the career ladder, for this type of adjustment.

Rosalyn Yalow, a Nobel prize winner in medicine, spoke out strongly in the 1970's about women and the problems that they can expect if they approach their professional assignments with any expectation of treatment different from that of men.[15] Her rather strong stand for equal oppor-tunity and equal responsibility for both sexes is exemplifed by the following statement:

> For instance, in discussions with women who wish to become physicians, I emphasize that an enormous investment in them is made by society, as well as by their families and themselves, in their training. They should accept this investment only if it is their intent to be full-time physicians. The request of some women's medical associations for part-time residencies for women during their child-bearing years is unwise and unfair. Of course, some women, and some men, will drop out of a particular field, but the percentage of women doing so should not be greater than that of men or it will hurt the cause of other women who aspire to that field.

Not every woman, nor man, for that matter, would agree with the stand taken by Rosalyn Yalow. Yet no one can deny that different treatment does emphasize differences and hin-ders the acceptance of the notion of equality. Using femi-ninity as an advantage in business dealings may damage the notion of equality of the sexes.

Sara Lou Brown, a partner with Peat, Marwick, Mitchell & Co., was interviewed in the 1970's as the first woman partner of one of the Big Eight accounting firms in Texas. She stated: "My attitude has been to avoid reminding people that I am a female. I would simply like to be successful as an accountant."[16]

Supervision of Women

Other types of problems were brought in by the new wave of women accountants. One is the supervision of the women themselves. G. Rayburn, a prolific author on the subject of women professionals, wrote the following in 1974:

> The human relations side of the supervisor's job is even more important in working with women. Women also seem to be more influenced than men by the work atmosphere. They are interested in the people who work with them and the people they work for. The supervisor has to be more tactful in reprimanding a woman, since she has a stronger need for approval and reassurance. Women take criticism harder than men. Praising the employee on a job well done is more important to women than it is to men. At the same time they are more willing to admit their mistakes, and they develop a sense of team spirit more easily.[17]

It would seem that a man who has been a good supervisor would be good regardless of whether he is in charge of men or women. However, some men who are excellent supervisors of men have failed in their duties of overseeing women. This is often due to a built-in prejudice about women. The supervisor may operate at the other extreme and fail to hold women to the same work standards that were applied to men. If he operates at either extreme, he is in for personnel trouble.

From another perspective, some claim that men who supervise women have an advantage over women who supervise men. This, they claim, is because women prefer a man boss. Perhaps the reasons for this belief lies deep within our culture. Since women throughout history had been raised to regard men as the natural supervisor, it was easier for them to take orders from a man. When these same women reached positions of leadership they faced a double-whammy. Now they had to supervise men, many of whom also thought that men were ordained to be the natural leader and therefore resisted women supervisors. At that point, professional expertise and technical knowledge became the woman's strongest tools, for her true power lay in what is generally called the "power of expertise." She knew how to get the job done, and this ability is strong medicine in professional circles, especially in one like public accounting, where time is short and time-budget overruns are disastrous.

A Matter of Title

Another small but significant problem associated with this new wave of women accountants was how to address them. During the 1970's the title "Ms." was utilized frequently, and in public accounting it appeared to be more common than in other business sectors. Some married women retained their maiden names while others did not, but in any case there appeared a preference in public accounting for the Ms. designation. Women had been accused of being more easily intimidated by clients than were men, and the retention of one's maiden name and the use of the Ms. designation evidently was considered a sign of self-confidence and self-assertiveness. In some firms it almost seemed that an apology was needed if a woman took her husband's name.

On the other hand, men not accustomed to introducing women as equals frequently misused titles in such a way as to be almost insulting; and in many other cases their introductions reflected a strong sex bias. For example, one female professional received a copy of a memo typed "copy to Mr. Smith, Mr. Jones, and Mary White." Most women accept either formal or informal terms, but when such differences exist in the form of reference, it is both frustrating and disrespectful.

This same problem has filtered down to female secretaries, who may answer the telephone for women. They may also be reluctant to do clerical chores for women but not for men professionals. Tension and jealousy can develop, since female secretaries may tend to treat female professionals more on a woman-to-woman basis than on a secretary-to-professional basis. This unfortunately often makes it necessary for women professionals to "keep a distance" from the female secretaries to dispel any ideas that her work comes last in the department or that her work is not as important as the men's. It becomes important that professional designations as well as personal ones be systematically and equally used for both men and women. The first wave of women in public accounting learned this early in the game.

Turnover

During the 1970's, most men in the profession held firmly to the belief that women were less career-minded, that they would not be willing to commit themselves to the profession, that they did not really have long-term career goals, and that these differences would be excessively costly to the profession in high turnover rates. Arguments on both sides of these questions were offered without sufficient evidence at that time to prove or disprove it. Personal bias predominated, and each person took whatever position supported his or her beliefs. Women, of course, steadfastly held that these were myths. As notable a person as Walter Mondale is quoted early in his political career as saying, "Everyone knows that women don't work for the same reasons as men."[18] He must have respected their reasons, whatever he perceived them to be for he selected Geraldine Ferraro as a running mate in his campaign for the Presidency. Perhaps he was basing this early quote on the misleading statistics and the myths that were generally accepted at the time. The numbers quoted in those days were based on the use of government statistics, which included the entire female work force and were therefore biased against women in managerial and professional positions. The statistics indicated that absenteeism and turnover were higher for both men and women in less skilled and lower paid jobs, and women were predominant in these lower groups. The statistics for men and women were therefore based on two different populations that were really not comparable. Few surveys have been made of absenteeism and turnover rates in jobs with educational requirements and responsibilities comparable to those existing in public accounting.

However, a few studies were available by the late 1970s, and they began to show a slightly higher turnover rate for women. It must be recognized that in a way these predicted higher turnover rates were a self-fulfilling prophecy. Since women accountants were thought to have a higher turnover rate, they were paid less than men, or were given less prestigious assignments, or were not promoted at the same rate as men. When the woman accountant found a job with equal pay or equal responsibilities, she changed jobs, thus proving the original assumption.

Professors Konstana and Ferris[19] undertook a longitudinal survey of turnover rates in 1981. From their results they concluded that during the first year of employment the turnover rate among female and male auditors was approximately the same. After this point, however, the termination rate among the female auditors began to outpace the male rate. By the end of the third year, the turnover rate for the sample of women was nearly twice the rate of the sample of men. Relative stability appeared to be reached sometime after the fourth year. On the basis of these data, it could be inferred that the public accounting firms studied did not or were not meeting the expectations or needs of their professional female staff. Given this inference, it is not surprising that the termination rate for females is higher at about the three-year point in public accounting employment.

This study, which included both men and women, found

that those who left were most dissatisfied with the training received from their superiors and with their opportunity to grow professionally, whereas those who stayed felt greater dissatisfaction with their opportunity to interact with partners and realize their professional goals. Only three significant differences were observed between those who left and those who stayed—those who left were (1) significantly more dissatisfied with the opportunity to work with friendly associates, (2) more dissatisfied with their opportunity to plan their job activities, and (3) significantly less dissatisfied with their firm's support of professional activities.

A study of the American Women's Society of CPA's concentrated solely on women, and the results reflect the strong feelings of inadequate opportunities. This study found that the three reasons given most frequently by women for leaving public accounting were:

1. Long overtime hours
2. Not being developed for future responsibilities
3. Better professional opportunities elsewhere

Many reasons other than these were given, but these three were the most frequent. It is most significant that the three reasons for leaving which are used so frequently to argue against hiring women appeared last on the list—to have children, husband transferred, and marriage. These were given as reasons for terminating by only 7 percent, 3 percent, and 2 percent, respectively, of the women contacted.[20] These findings show rather conclusively that the self-fulfilling prophecy is indeed at work.

By the end of the 1970's many of the problems discussed in this chapter had become old-hat. Firms through established policy and individuals through experience had learned how to handle the problems originally encountered when women entered the profession in appreciable numbers. Many unresolved issues remain, to be sure, and many barriers still exist, but women are now an integral and indispensable force within the professional community. Judy Walsh, one of those who entered the profession in this early period and stayed to become a partner with one of the largest and most prestigious firms, Deloitte, Haskins and Sells, gave this advice:

> Accounting requires aptitudes and skills which are neither masculine nor feminine, and it offers a wide variety of specialties, all of which should be considered open to women. The opportunities for women at Haskins and Sells are expanding, due in large part to the success of those who have been with the firm so far. They are a bright, positive and dynamic group who, when they encountered obstacles, found ways to deal with them.
>
> Do the job as well as possible. Be willing and able to take all the pressures a man will have to take. Be a lady but don't be overly emotional or sensitive; be a true professional in appearance and in behavior; and most important, maintain your sense of humor and roll with the punches.[21]

Sara Lou Brown, a partner with the firm of Peat, Marwick, Mitchell & Co. is an example of one of those women who joined the profession with the first wave. She is a tax partner in her native Houston office, and her story is typical of the first women to break into the modern-day profession.

Sara Lou Brown was a very good student while in high school, graduating 13th in a class of 1,600 students, with a heavy math and science emphasis. When she enrolled at Rice University, an elite university of Ivy League caliber, she took an introductory accounting course and enjoyed it. She had decided not to try for an engineering career and knew there was little future in being a math or a liberal arts major. When she found that she did well in accounting and liked it, she saw a possibility there for a meaningful career. She graduated in 1964, having decided to go into public accounting. Two of the large Big Eight firms, but none of the smaller local firms, granted her an employment interview. She knows now, but did not know then, that these two interviews were more for show than for real. In spite of her exceptional academic record, she did not receive an employment offer from either of them. At that time they did not really want women.

Like many of the determined women who could not get employment which would provide the necessary experience to sit for the CPA exam, she went on to graduate studies. In the Fall of 1964 she enrolled in the Master of Business Administration program at the University of Texas in Austin. I was her advisor in that program and had her in my graduate classes. There were two women who enrolled in my classes during those two years—Sara Lou Brown and a young woman named Mary Ann Harris. There were some forty to fifty students in each class, and these two young women were very visible among the room full of men. The two led the class, each with excellent grades. They knew that if they were to have a chance at a job offer from one of the public accounting firms they would have to be better than just good; they would have to be excellent—and they were.

I lost track of Mary Ann Harris; she went to Dallas with one of the Big Eight accounting firms there. She was their first woman staff member. But Sara Lou Brown went to Houston with Peat, Marwick, Mitchell & Co. and has been with them ever since. Upon completion of the Master's degree she interviewed with one of the two firms that had granted her an interview two years earlier. Times had changed, and the firm needed new staff. Now that she had a graduate degree they decided to make her an offer, which she accepted, and she and one other woman from another university started to work for the firm. This was to be the start of the new wave of women in that firm, but at the time Sara Lou did not know that. How could she? She was, however, well aware of the fact that she was breaking new ground.

The firm placed both of the women in the tax department. As Sara Lou phrased it, "They wanted us there so that we would not be visible to the clients." There were some thirty professionals in the tax area of the Houston office of the firm at that time, and having not one but *two* women was most unusual. The other woman stayed eight years before leaving the firm to start her own practice. Sara Lou Brown remained at the firm and has been a partner now for some twelve years.

Having exceptional abilities, she was promoted through the ranks rapidly. According to her account, she was in the right place at the right time. The firm's tax practice was expanding rapidly, and they needed competent persons at the management level. The rate of growth of this particular practice office was 20 percent per year, placing tremendous strain on the existing partners and managers. She moved up rapidly.

She considers herself more inclined toward people than number-oriented activities, and she possesses excellent interpersonal and managerial skills. She said, "I would say that in our firm an inability to work well with people is the primary reason for a senior manager being denied a partnership. Our tax department has a training program which includes required coverage in people skills, since that is one of the areas of weakness of many people. I'm not certain whether these skills can be learned, though; for if they do not exist by the time a person is thirty years old, it becomes very difficult to develop them. But we do all we can."

Sara Lou Brown is not a "women's libber." Though she comes across as being feminine, she tends to play down her femininity in the work environment, preferring instead to emphasize her professional competencies. She has not participated in the activities of women's organizations, believing that they tend to call attention to differences, but she is active in the national, state, and local professional societies. This reflects her confidence; she is not afraid to compete with men in a man's world.

As a partner she has somewhat more control over her schedule than staff persons do, and like many women in public accounting, she waited until her career was established before starting her family. Her son Dereck was born after she had been a partner for several years. But even with a very comfortable income and an established career, she acknowledges that there are still problems in balancing a career with a family. Competent help to care for the child, who is going on eight, is difficult to find.

In spite of the family demands and the heavy work schedule, she still finds time for outside activities. She gives generously of her exceptional talents to the community, especially to universities and colleges in the Houston area. She serves on several boards and councils at Rice University and at the Houston Community College. She is especially active in the alumni activities of her alma mater, and at one time served as an officer of the Houston Grand Opera.

Sara Lou Brown came into the profession when women were being admitted "on trial," and she was one of that first wave to prove herself. There are dozens like her, and though not all can be identified, since time has erased their trails, the profession must recognize here the heritage it has received from them.

REFERENCES

1. Sandstrom, A., "Are Women Keeping Pace?" *The Woman CPA,* Vol. 25, No. 6, October, 1963, pp. 3–5.
2. Epstein, C. *Women in Law,* Anchor Press, Garden City, New York, 1983, p. 4.
3. Brown, J., "Women Auditors—A Quiet Invasion into the Male World," *Government Accountant's Journal,* Spring, 1981, pp. 24–27.
4. Epstein, op. cit., p. 5.
5. "Accounting for Women," *Lybrand Journal,* Vol. 53, Fall, 1972, pp. 37–44.
6. Walsh, Judy, written up in "Well, You Don't Look Like an Accountant," *H & S Reports,* Vol. 11, No. 4, Autumn, 1974, pp. 20–23.
7. Krause, K., "Women CPA's—One Firm's Experience," *The Practicing CPA,* American Institute of Certified Public Accountants, Vol. 8, No. 4, April, 1984, pp. 1–2.
8. McCoy, D., "Lipstick, Nylons and CPA's," *The Nebraska CPA,* Vol. 5, No. 2, Fall, 1960, p. 21.
9. Devine, D., "A Career in Industry: A Female Perspective," *Pennsylvania CPA Spokesman,* Vol. 52, No. 3, November, 1981, pp. 14–15. This has been reprinted

with permission from the PENNSYLVANIA CPA JOURNAL, a publication of the Pennsylvania Institute of Certified Public Accountants.

10. "The Accountant is a Woman," *Ernst and Ernst,* Vol. 11, No. 2, Summer, 1972.

11. Rayburn, L., "Subtle Discrimination within the Accounting Profession," *The Georgia CPA,* Vol. 14, No. 4, 1972–73, pp. 10–14.

12. "Accustomed to Her Face," *H & S Reports,* Vol. 8, No. 1, Winter, 1971, pp. 20–23.

13. Subosits, C., "Women in Major CPA Firms—A Reflection," *Pennsylvania CPA Spokesman,* Vol. 52, No. 3, November, 1981, pp. 7–8.

14. Shern, S., "A Woman CPA Looks at Public Accounting," *Management Accounting,* Vol. 61, No. 8, February, 1980, pp. 39–43.

15. Yalow, R., "A Winner (Nobel Prize) Talks about the Status of Her Sex," *Across the Board, The Conference Board Magazine,* Vol. 16, No. 9, September, 1979, pp. 54–59.

16. Harvison, J., "Women CPA's Come of Age," *Texas Society of CPA's News,* Vol. 1, No. 6, January, 1975, pp. 9–10.

17. Rayburn, L. G., "The Woman Accountant as an Asset to the Accounting Profession," *The National Public Accountant,* Vol. 29, October, 1974, pp. 12–16.

18. *The Los Angeles Times,* Oct. 23, 1970.

19. Konstana, C., and Ferris, K., "Female Turnover in Professional Accounting Firms: Some Preliminary Findings," *The Michigan CPA,* Winter, 1981, pp. 11–15.

20. Walkup, N. and Fenzau, D., "Women CPA's: Why They Leave Public Accounting," *The Woman CPA,* Vol. 42, October, 1980, pp. 3–6.

21. Walsh, Judy, op. cit.

Preparing for the Profession

Most new entrants into the public accounting profession come from university accounting programs. The majority of them have attended the usual four-year programs, graduating with Bachelor's degrees. In spite of their accounting orientation, students generally know very little about public accounting when they begin interviewing for jobs. Their professional training has given them a strong technical foundation upon which to begin their careers, but for the most part they have limited insight into the realities of public accounting. At best they have only a vague idea of the advantages and disadvantages of large versus small firms, the Big Eight versus local firms, or audit versus tax and consulting specialties.

Information Sources

One of the factors that contribute to the lack of information in this regard is that professors and counselors themselves are generally not fully knowledgeable about all the possibilities, and some are reluctant to make definite statements about advantages and disadvantages. The practicing profession is very close to the university faculty, providing many types of support to the educational process. If the professor's discussion of advantages and disadvantages is misunderstood by the student, and word gets back to one of the Big Eight firms that "Professor Jones said that local firms provide better working conditions," Professor Jones is put in an embarrassing position with that Big Eight firm.

While most professors do try to counsel their students, usually the discussion concerns some of the less important aspects, such as training facilities, work hours, pay scale differences, and the length of time for advancement. Since these factors differ from firm to firm, the professor or counselor must be careful not to insert personal biases or be too specific. More than once a recruiter has remarked that a student said, "Professor Jones told the class such-and-such," when we knew from experience that Jones held the opposite view. Misunderstandings and misinterpretations are highly probable in this type of counseling.

A great deal of the information received by students concerning the advantages or disadvantages of working with a particular firm comes from friends and acquaintances and is usually very biased. Teresa Bonario, a senior in her last semester and just beginning the interview process, said to us as we gathered data for this book, "I think a smaller firm is better. Even though the training in a Big Eight firm is better, it is more concentrated. I would not be able to branch out with a big firm and learn more about different types of businesses. Also, I think that it is easier to develop relationships with co-workers and supervisors in a small firm, and there is a better chance for advancement."

These same arguments could be turned around and used in just the opposite way—large firms have a broader client base, provide more, rather than less, diversification, their training programs are better, etc. When asked where she heard these things, Teresa replied that her friend who graduated last semester told her. Whether the information was right or wrong will depend upon her own personality and career objectives. The point is that students must make career choices with imperfect information, and unfortunately all too often the choices are not correct for that student.

The Market

A high rate of employee turnover is endemic to public accounting. The long overtime hours and the stress associated with a constant series of deadlines produce a state of burnout after two or three years in the profession. In fact, there is a frequently used phrase called the "three-year burnout," although it is sometimes altered to the "five-year burnout." In most of the large firms the turnover rate approaches 50 percent after three years, and at five years may be as high as 70 percent. This high rate means that only one in five new staff members hired in any given year are expected to be with that same firm five years later. Of the four who leave, some will move to accounting positions with industry or government, but very often they take positions with client companies whose personnel, operations, and financial affairs are well known to the departing CPA. After all, he or she has worked as an auditor or consultant for that firm for several years. The value of the years of experience which the individual has had with the ex-public accounting firm should not be underestimated. The new position may be as controller or treasurer with a former client, at a salary and with responsibilities far in excess of what might have been possible otherwise. Public accounting is the greatest springboard to high-level financial careers available anywhere in today's world.

Given the constant turnover of departing CPA's, the ranks of the practicing firms would be depleted were it not for the unceasing stream of new entrants. Thus public accounting firms are the most consistent and the most active recruiters visiting college campuses today. A single large international CPA firm will frequently come to a campus that has 150 to 200 young men and women graduating from accounting programs, interview at least half of them, and then extend employment offers to half of those interviewed. It is not at all unusual for a single office in a fairly large city to have a hiring goal of several hundred new recruits each year—just to fill the ranks of those who have left. If the firm is growing, the demand is even greater.

The current demand for new recruits is almost insatiable. In fact, the beginning stages of this strong need for large numbers of recruits played a major role in opening the profession to women some fifteen years ago. Women are now recruited as enthusiastically as men, and almost equal numbers of each are hired every year. The larger firms have recruiting specialists in each of their offices who coordinate the recruiting process, and these specialists have sizeable staffs of assistants to help carry out the interviewing process.

Big Eight Recruiting

Almost all of the larger firms have slick brochures and fancy booklets prepared and distributed by the thousands which tell students the advantages of coming to work for their firm. The thirty-six page brochure prepared by Touche Ross to recruit for their consulting activities contains these opening paragraphs, typical of those appearing in the profession's recruiting literature.

> At Touche Ross, we have developed one of the nation's most respected, most diversified, and fastest-growing management consulting practices. We are now looking for candidates who can join our approximately 500 highly qualified professionals in becoming agents of change in industry, in government, and in our social institutions. This brochure will help you to determine whether the style, the pace, and the breadth of management consulting at Touche Ross will enable you to meet your own career goals. Does Touche Ross offer the right challenge, the right career, the right firm—for you?
>
> To reach a valid judgment about Touche Ross' management consulting practice, you need some facts. Evaluate the information to follow in the context of

your personal capabilities and ambitions. Then, take a look at the career consultants who are profiled in this brochure. As they describe their own satisfactions— not without reservations—they may help you to make your own choice of a firm. Certainly they represent the highly qualified professionals who are now following their career paths at Touche Ross, but, equally, they represent the type of person we are seeking.[1]

The brochure gives profiles of several individuals, with photos showing them as interesting people leading interesting lives. Carol McElyea, a Chicago partner, is one of the several featured. In addition to a professional work-related photo, her trim, athletic figure is also shown as she competes in a racquetball game. The message in this brochure says very clearly that the recruit's life with the firm will be interesting and rewarding.

The Campus Visit

Over 500 universities provide graduating students for new staff positions. The recruiters set their itinerary of schools to be visited months in advance and do all they can to alert students to the days that they will be on campus. Early in the Fall, usually in October, they begin their invasion of the campuses. As many as a dozen recruiters from a single firm will appear at the larger universities, staying two or three days to complete their initial screening of students. The usual arrangement is a thirty-minute interview, with one student and one interviewer shut up in a small cubbyhole. Prior to the 1970's women were frequently discouraged from taking up the interviewer's time, since their chance of being hired was small, if indeed there was any chance at all.

Even today the biases of the individual interviewer can place the student at a disadvantage. This possible mismatch applies to both men and women, though the ghosts of old prejudices make it less likely for men. To increase the odds, most students sign up for interviews with four or five different firms, some with as many as ten firms. Most students with good grade point averages and reasonably good personalities will survive this initial screening and receive invitations for the next step—an office visit.

Several weeks after a campus interview the selected students receive letters inviting them to visit the nearest practice office. Some of the better students receive invitations from all of the firms they interviewed, while others may receive only one or two invitations, and the weaker students may receive none. These weaker students may have to change their career goals and consider jobs with industry or government, or they may go out "on the streets" visiting local practitioners or answering classified ads for accountants. This painful process of scaling down expectations is necessary for the tail-end of the class.

The period between interviews and receipt of the office invitation letters is a very anxious time, especially for those whose grades were not strong. It is well known around the campus that students with less than a B average may not survive the interview process with the more prestigious firms, and unless they have something else going for them, they may not receive an invitation for an office visit. Being active on campus, holding a position such as class president, being editor of the school paper, or being a star football player sometimes offsets a less than B average, but generally public accountants look for good minds coupled with a willingness to work. A strong grade point average is the best measure of this.

The Office Visit

The office visit provides the student an opportunity to look over the facilities and meet with partners and staff. It provides those who do the hiring with enough information to make an intelligent decision on whether an employment offer should be extended. Lunch with some of the firm's personnel provides a means of measuring the recruit's ability to converse and an adeptness with the social graces. The office visits are arranged on an individual basis, so that each recruit is on his or her own. The firm's partners want to see an ability to handle oneself without the support of a group. The office visit, which for some is quite stressful, is the last step in the employment process, and those who are selected receive offer letters within a month or so. Some might receive an offer right on the spot, if the partners see outstanding potential.

Characteristics Recruiters Look For

A group of interviewers were asked in a recent study to rank fifteen characteristics which they examine in the hiring process.[2] These fifteen items were ranked in order of importance, first as they apply to the campus interview and, second, as they apply to the office interview.

RANKING OF PERSONAL CHARACTERISTICS

FOR HIRING COLLEGE GRADUATES

	During a Campus interview	During the Office Visit
Accounting grade point average	1	6
Overall grade point average	2	7
Self-confidence/assertiveness	3	1
Interpersonal skills	4	3
Intelligence	5	5
Involvement in outside activities	6	11
Involvement in campus activities	7	12
Work experience—accounting	8	8
Motivation/ambition	9	2
Verbal skills	10	4
Work experience—non-accounting	11	13
Knowledge of the firm	12	14
Knowledge of public accounting	13	9
Appearance	14	15
Analytical skills	15	10

This study emphasizes that the initial interview is a screening based primarily on mental abilities and skills. Grade point averages and self-confidence are the prime characteristics at that point. It is interesting that appearance falls in 14th place. However, most students attempt to dress in a very professional fashion for their interviews. It may be that professional appearance is accepted as a given, and recuiters are looking for qualities that will distinguish the recruit as an individual.

During the office visit, however, the screening shifts toward the individual's personality characteristics. Self-confidence/assertiveness and motivation/ambition are the traits given first and second priority, with interpersonal and verbal skills not far behind. These traits are difficult to assess during a thirty minute campus interview, but during an all-day office visit there is time to assess them adequately.

Academic Qualifications

Recruiters do not generally give favorable marks to students with grades below 3.0, or a B average. To acquire a 3.0 average a student must have at least one A (exceptional performance) for each C (average performance). Only about one in every three students who graduate in accounting can maintain such an average. In some universities, grades are tougher to earn, and perhaps only one in five will have such an average. Recruiters know which universities give higher grading scales and factor this knowledge into their selection process.

In addition to the grade-point average, recruiters scrutinize the grades that a student is able to earn in certain accounting courses. Most accounting programs on a semester basis system require eight to ten separate courses in accounting, while those in a trimester system may require fifteen shorter courses. Without a high grade-point average in these key accounting courses, the student does not offer much promise of being successful in the accounting profession, and recruiters place heavy weight on this fact.

Although campus recruiting is the primary source of new entrants to the profession, a considerable recruiting effort goes on outside the campus. Smaller firms looking for only one or two new staff members will frequently advertise in the professional section of the employment want-ads. Employment agencies and head-hunters are frequently used also, and both experienced public accountants and inexperienced students are able to locate suitable positions through these avenues. However, campus recuiting will continue to be the method through which the vast majority of new staff is located and hired.

Personality Differences

The need for a new army of recruits each year has entirely removed the reluctance once so evident in the recruiting and hiring of women. Enough experience has now been gained to make meaningful comparisons between women and men students who select accounting as a career and between men and women on the staff of public accounting firms. In a 1978 study appearing in *The Woman CPA,*[3] Adlayn Frasier and her co-authors compared the academic performance of female and male accounting majors and found that women performed somewhat better than males in undergraduate accounting courses. They also examined personality differences between female and male accounting students, using the Edwards Personality Preference Schedule, and found that, of the fifteen characteristics measured, significant differences existed for six. They concluded, "Women in accounting do differ, however, in some important respects from other college women. They have higher needs for achievement and for order, and have more endurance relative to other college-age women." This study was administered to over 100 women seniors who were preparing for accounting careers and also to a significant number of women CPA's in practice. The results reflect some interesting traits about women who select accounting as their major subject in college.

Achievement. The women accounting students tested revealed a significantly higher achievement need than their college-age counterparts. Accounting study seems to have attracted those who aspire to higher achievement.

Deference. This trait measures one's need to get input, to seek advice, to elicit suggestions, and accept orders from others. Women accounting students showed significantly *less* deference than did other college women.

Order. The need for order was significantly higher in the accounting group than for other women students.

Exhibition. This trait measures the need to be noticed, to stand out, and to be the center of attraction. College students studying accounting did not differ from other college women in this respect, but did have a greater amount of this trait than practicing women CPA's. Perhaps age and experience produced this difference.

Affiliation. This trait measures the need to be associated with other people. Accounting women students had less of this trait than other college women which may indicate that women accountants are more independent in judgment.

Intraception. This trait measures the need to analyze the motives for one's own actions or thoughts, and also those of others. Women studying accounting were significantly *lower* than other women on this scale. They tend to accept at face value and not search for underlying or hidden motives.

Succorance. This is the need to receive support and encouragement from others. Accounting women students did not have more or less of this characteristic than other women college students, but did have less than practicing CPA's. The practicing woman CPA evidently does not need as much of the "pat on the back," perhaps because she has reached a higher level of self-confidence and maturity.

Abasement. This is the need to accept self-blame and assume full responsibility for the outcome of events, rather than placing responsibility on an outside source. Women accounting students had less of this trait than other women in the study.

Nurturance. This is the need to give support. Women accounting students reported lower scores than other women on campus, but the same as practicing women CPA's.

Endurance. This trait is especially important in accounting, due to the long overtime hours often required. Women accounting students scored *higher* than other women students, but *lower* than practicing women CPA's, indicating that the ranks of the practicing CPA's had been purged of those who did not have strength in this trait.

Heterosexuality. The need to be with the opposite sex was not different for any of the groups in the study.

Aggression. This category measures the need to attack contrary points of view and the need to argue. No significant differences in this trait were found.

Based upon the results of this study, one can conclude that the women who select accounting as their major subject in college are high achievers, demonstrating greater than average qualities of orderliness, intraception, and endurance, and with lower tendencies toward deference, affiliation, and abasement. One hardly sees the "clinging vine" or the "can't make up her mind" woman in this picture. It does show a self-assured person not afraid to make hard decisions when the need arises.

Another study of a similar nature was completed in 1982 that compared women and men accounting students. This study utilized the Self-Description Inventory, a frequently used measure which relates personality traits with managerial ability.[4] Twelve traits are measured when this instrument is used, and, since a different number of questions are used to measure each trait, the scales for all twelve traits do not have the same numerical totals. The women/men comparison was as follows:

	Men	**Women**	
Supervisory ability	26.12	26.82	*
Occupational achievement	32.89	33.98	*
Intelligence	36.01	37.58	*
Self-actualization	10.24	10.12	
Self-assurance	24.07	24.14	*
Decisiveness	18.48	18.22	
Need for security	14.32	14.22	*!
Working class affinity	14.52	14.30	*!
Initiative	28.51	27.46	
Need for high financial reward	6.89	6.68	*!
Need for power	11.10	11.48	*
Maturity	28.18	28.10	

* = Mean is higher for females than for males
! = Negatively related to managerial talent

The comparison of the male/female differences shows clearly that women accounting students had scores that indicated stronger managerial potential on eight of the twelve traits. Three of these traits have negative correlations with managerial talents, and on all three of these the scores of the women students were lower (more favorable) than the scores of the men students.

Grade Differences

There is another difference between the women who study accounting and their male classmates. *Women consistently make higher grades in accounting classes.* There are exceptions, of course, and we can speak only in generalities and work with average grades, but over the years our own personal experiences have been that in most cases women students will lead the class. Art Hendricks, former managing partner of a large international CPA firm and now an educator, studied the grade point averages of men and women accounting students at two widely separated large state universities.[5] He found that the average of grades earned by women in his sample was 3.1, as compared with a 2.5 for men. (An A is 4.0, B is 3.0, and C is 2.0.) Hendricks also found that during the years covered by his study, 60 percent of the accounting classes were men and 40 percent were women, with little deviation from this mix from one class to another. He also found that the 40 percent made up of women earned 64 percent of the A grades which are normally given for exceptional performance.

Weston and Maloney analyzed the grades at another university and reported the following:[6]

Grade Point Average	Male	Female
3.5 and above	23%	65%
3.0 to 3.49	35%	18%
2.5 to 2.99	17%	12%
below 2.5	25%	5%

Why Accounting?

Weston and Maloney also surveyed both men and women students to determine why they chose accounting as their primary area of concentration. The students were asked to rank eight factors in the order of their influence in the decision to study accounting.

RANKING OF FACTORS INFLUENCING THE CHOICE OF
ACCOUNTING AS A MAJOR

Men	Women
1. Salary potential	1. Availability of jobs
2. Courses interesting and challenging	2. Courses interesting and challenging
3. Availability of jobs	3. Quantitative orientation aptitude with numbers
4. Desire for a specialized business background	4. Salary potential
5. Quantitative orientation aptitude with numbers	5. Desire for a specialized business background
6. Influence of family member or friend	6. Influence of family member or friend
7. Prestige of professional status	7. Encouragement of teacher or guidance counselor
8. Encouragement of teacher or guidance counselor	8. Prestige of professional status

Only two of the eight factors involved in deciding upon a career in accounting were ranked equally by the men and women. They gave equal rankings to the extent of the influence of family members and friends and the fact that they found their accounting courses interesting and challenging. However, the number one factor for women was *availability of jobs,* while men were more heavily swayed by salary potential. Prestige of professional status appeared to be one of the lesser weighted factors for both men and women students. The value of this factor emerges and grows as one spends more time in the professional ranks, and students have not as yet assumed a professional stance. Those already in a profession, whether it be law, medicine, or accounting, would undoubtedly give more weight to this dimension.

Changes in Educational Process

The AICPA, as the national professional organization, has a vital interest in the educational process and periodically studies the educational requirements for entry into the profession. Every five or ten years the AICPA appoints a commission, a council, or a committee to restudy the educational requirements and make recommendations for improvement of college accounting programs. While the recommendations of these groups can be considered only as advice to universities, they are given serious consideration. The last formal report of the AICPA in this regard was issued in 1978 and was entitled *Educational Requirements for Entry Into the Accounting Profession.*[7] This report called for a five-year university accounting program, adding a fifth year to the normal four-year undergraduate program. To date, however, only a fraction of the universities throughout the country has set up such programs, others showing strong resistance to breaking the tradition of a four-year college program.

Graduate degrees in accounting appear to be more popular than the fifth year at the undergraduate level. Recruiters enthusiastically search out students who will receive graduate degrees in accounting, because these individuals have not only graduate training, but also fairly high grade point averages. Entrance into graduate programs requires at least a B average, and the maturity that comes with graduate studies is highly desirable from the standpoint of the hiring firm. Graduate studies provide more insight into the complexities of the profession and the political processes that exert an influence upon the profession. For these reasons, starting salaries of students receiving Master's degrees are from two to five thousand dollars per year higher than starting salaries of students receiving baccalaureate degrees.

Job Preferences

Although a sizeable proportion of women students with the proper credentials hope to begin their careers with one of the large international firms, an equally large group does not. Whether this proportion differs between men and women is not known, but in a study by J. Lambert and S. Lambert, a combined group of men and women students expressed the following preferences.[8] (Note that this study relates to job offers which the students would *not accept* if received from that source.)

**PERCENT OF STUDENTS WHO WOULD NOT
ACCEPT A JOB OFFER FROM:**

City, County, or State Government	60%
Industry	58%
Large international CPA firm	52%
Federal government	48%
Regional CPA firm	32%
Local CPA firm	28%

Local governments were the least desired employers, probably because of low pay scales and few opportunities for advancement. Industry followed closely behind. Only about half of the students would have accepted employment offers from large international CPA firms, with the federal government not far ahead. The most acceptable employers were the regional and local CPA firms. A much smaller proportion of the students would not take a job with this type of firm if such a job became available.

These statistics must be taken with a grain of salt. Realistically, a student would take a job with any of these *if it were the only job available*. The students were in effect expressing a type of negative preference; that is, "I would not accept an offer from the federal government, provided one were available to me from a local or regional CPA firm." However, at least some idea of preferences is available from these data.

Woman Recruiters

With women becoming a more substantial part of the profession, their involvement in the recruiting process was inevitable. More and more women are appearing with the recruiting teams on campuses, and they are very effective recruiters. But some problems still exist when women interview men, in somewhat similar fashion to the early days when men recruiters began recruiting women.

In the mid-to-late 1970's a few firms began to place women on their interview teams. The firms' managements were not sure what degree of acceptance would be forthcoming, and the effectiveness of these women was carefully monitored. A study of their performance was made at that time, and the results indicated that in general they were better interviewers than men.[9]

When asked to compare female recruiters with their male counterparts, 80 percent of the women rated female recruiters better than or equal to male recruiters. Female interviewers were variously described by these students as "more efficient," "more genuinely interested in me," "much more probing," "more honest, open, and receptive," and "definitely the most professional." Five out of six men regarded women interviewers as equal to or better than a male interviewer. The one out of six who did not like women interviewers expressed the feeling that he was not comfortable with a woman. One of these said, "I do not feel any woman should interview men. I feel that I was put in an uneasy position from the start." Perhaps he felt uneasy as a result of prejudice, or perhaps as a result of an overinflated ego. In any case, his response reflects the lingering reluctance some men have to a woman interviewer.

Interviewing is a two-way street. Each person makes an impression on the other, but the interviewee has more to lose and is in a more stressful position. In a recent study of interviewers from national CPA firms, Margaret Prather and Paul Dierks investigated the interviewer's impressions of men and women interviewees.[10] They were asked if they found any significant difference between men and women in the area of nonverbal communication (i.e., nervous habits, body language). Most reported that women have better verbal and communications skills and dress more appropriately for the interview than do men. The interviewers were asked whether age is more of a factor for women than for men. Several recruiters felt that women with heavy family responsibilities shied away from the large accounting firms because they were aware of the greater potential conflicts between family demands and the requirements of a position with that kind of firm. However, each recruiter emphatically stated that the presence of young children at home would not prevent a woman from obtaining a position with their firm or advancing within the organization.

The recruiters felt women were clearly career-oriented. However they felt that women's planning horizons tended to be shorter than men's. Also, in spite of the findings of some earlier studies, the recruiters felt that women students were not fully aware of the potential problems of discrimination in job advancement and interpersonal relations. Those who were aware, however, tended to take a very direct approach in inquiring about these items during the interview process.

Advice for Women

The final question asked of the recruiters in the study cited above was what advice they would give to a woman accounting student who was preparing to enter the job market, relative to how she could enhance herself and her interview skills. There were diverse answers to this question, but several common items appeared. For example, accounting grades are important, and every effort should be made to keep grades as high as possible; however, the student should not completely bury herself in her studies. Involvement in extracurricular activities, especially in a leadership position, and accounting-related work experience were also given importance. These are all tangible signs of intelligence, motivation, and ability.

As far as personal characteristics are concerned, knowing herself, her goals, and having the self-confidence and ability to describe them to someone else were stated by almost every recruiter as important personal characteristics. The development of an operating style, a presence, or an air of bearing, was considered important as long as the style fit the individual and her personality. Being honest, being able to express herself, and showing some ambition and motivation were also important.

One recruiter felt women needed to examine their ability to be assertive, to communicate to others their right to make reasonable requests, and to be themselves without making excuses. He felt this was far more important than being aggressive, which for women is often viewed in the negative sense. In our interviewing for this book most women students perceived that being themselves, without excuses or pretense, was of primary importance. Judith Blissard, a senior at a large state university who was just beginning the interview process, expressed this view clearly in her discussions with us. She had attended several of the monthly meetings of a large (over 500 persons) local chapter of CPA's. A recruiter for one of the Big Eight firms who was recruiting her had invited her to these meetings. She went to find out what the people in the profession were like. "One thing I noticed right off was that the women in accounting seem to be far more dynamic than the men," she said, "particularly the younger women." When asked to give her opinion on why this might be so, she replied, "I think accounting has drawn the brighter women. In the past women went into other professions, but I think today they see a challenge in accounting, and they see the opportunities which are there. I think the men see the profession as an opportunity, but not as a challenge and a frontier, as the brighter women do. As a result, the women are more enthusiastic, more interested, and more outgoing." When asked whether this outgoingness took these young women out of the conservative mold in which most people categorize accountants, she replied, "Yes, they are not conservative as persons, but they are as professionals. This may seem like a contradiction, but I don't see it that way. They are all personable, outgoing and enthusiastic, even though they all wear the same kind of suits, like they were cut out of a cookie-cutter. They have to compete with men professionally, but they are individuals, and they do not let their professionalism get in the way of being their own persons."

REFERENCES

1. Touche Ross & Co., *IF,* A recruiting brochure with copy and photos by David Dworsky, but without date.
2. Fraser, A., Lytle, R., and Stolle, C., "Profile of Female Accounting Majors, *"The Woman CPA,* Vol. 40, No. 4, October, 1978, pp. 18–21.
3. Fraser, A., Lytle, R., and Stolle, C., op. cit.
4. Cumpstopne, E., Dixon, B., and Taylor, D., "Female and Male Accounting Students," *The Woman CPA,* Vol. 44, April, 1982, pp. 8–11.
5. Hendricks, A., "Hiring the Woman Graduate: Why and How," *The National Public Accountant,* October, 1978, pp. 14–16.
6. Weston, M. and Maloney, J., "More College Women Majoring in Accounting: The Numbers and Some Reasons," *The Woman CPA,* Vol. 38, No. 1, January, 1976, pp. 14–22.
7. American Institute of Certified Public Accountants, *Educational Requirements for Entry Into the Profession,* New York, 1978.

8. Lambert, J., and Lambert S., "Attitudes and Expectations of Women Accounting Majors Toward Employment in Accounting," *The Nebraska CPA,* Vol. 9, No. 2, Fall, 1974, pp. 13–15.

9. Driscoll, J. and Hess, H., "The Recruiter: Woman's Friend or Foe?" *Journal of College Placement,* Vol. 34, Summer, 1974, pp. 32–34.

10. Prather, M. and Dierks, P., "Women in Job Interviews with Public Accounting Firms," *The Woman CPA,* Vol. 42, April, 1980, pp. 22–25.

Moving Up the Ladder

The normal progression of the young woman accountant as she moves up the career ladder is from staff to senior to manager, and it is hoped from there to full partnership. Becoming a partner in the firm is the ultimate goal, which for some becomes an obsession as the years in the manager position increase. The larger firms have formal promotions to the senior, manager, and partner positions, and their annual promotion lists are eagerly awaited.

A new entrant into the profession will normally be a staff person for two to three years before being promoted to senior. Some firms speak of seniors in terms of semi-seniors, seniors, and heavy seniors, although these sub-classifications are not usually formalized. A senior will normally remain in that category for three to four years before being moved up to manager. Again, there may be light managers, managers, and heavy managers, which are also informal designations. A period of four to five years is the normal amount of time spent as a manager before moving up to the partnership level. Overall, the time elapsed from the point of entrance as a new staff member to being admitted to partnership ranges from nine to eleven years in the larger national firms, but may occur more quickly in smaller local firms, since these firms do not formalize the promotion process quite so rigidly.

Only a handful of the thousands who enter the profession each year will reach the level of partner. The high dropout rate is due to several factors. Extremely heavy demands are placed upon the individual's time and energy, and many lack the personality characteristics needed for success. Those who withdraw from public accounting are still accountants, and they also retain their designation as a CPA. They typically leave active public practice to take positions as financial executives in industry, and a few take positions in government or in university teaching. They remain members of the same professional organizations and maintain close contact with those who continue in active public practice.

Initial Training

In the larger national firms, the first month or so on the job is spent in formal training programs. There is a series of such programs, ranging in length from one or two days to several weeks, and the first ones are usually held at the local facilities of the firm. In addition, the largest firms have training programs at the firm's national offices, and the new staff member may be in these programs for an additional two weeks of his or her first month on the job.

In the small local firms, the training is not as intense and assumes a more "on-the-job" nature. Smaller firms cannot afford elaborate training facilities such as the national firms have, but the smaller firms do utilize common training programs. A common training program arrangement permits a local firm to send one or two new staff members to a national or regional training program, where they study with new staff members from other local firms.

A staff accountant with a small, two-partner firm in Albuquerque commented on her firm's training this way: "My firm has a policy of providing at least forty hours of continuing professional education (each year) for all professional staff, whether certified or not. They stress training for the new, inexperienced staff accountants to help us develop into effective seniors, supervisors, and managers. And we get a lot of on-the-job help from the partners and managers to supplement the formal education. The firm's emphasis on training contributes to the reason we're highly respected in our area."

The basic duty of the new "junior accountant" is to do whatever the senior tells him or her to do. This may seem like a trite statement but it is close to the truth. Those exact words appear in a book entitled *The Duties of Junior and Senior Accountants,* published by the AICPA some years back.[1] Basically the new staff person is in a training position, learning to be a senior. Seniors are those who are in charge of the field work during an audit or a consulting engagement, or who complete tax assignments to the point that the work is ready for final review by a manager or partner. The junior during the first year does a great deal of "grunt work," which in the profession is commonly called "ticking and turning," a phrase which comes from having to examine documents for authenticity and correctness. In addition, it is well known that most staff quickly become experts at operating the copying machine.

Staff members also do a lot of inventory verification work. This requires checking the client's counts of various inventory items to insure that the inventory count and valuation are correct. In the first chapter of this book we quoted Carol Subosits, who was assigned a tour of coal mines, a midnight count of inventories at an aluminum mill, a chase of forklifts at a steel mill, a climb up silos, and a test count of explosives. These are the daily assignments of staff as they learn the process of inventory verification. One of the early objections that male auditors had to bringing women into the profession was that they would not be able to do these tasks—but women today are certainly as adept as men at carrying out such assignments.

Reflecting the Right Image

Perhaps the most basic education that new staff receive is not given in formal programs. The informal training in office protocol, or how to conduct one's self at the client's offices as well as at one's own, in dress codes, and in maintaining a professional bearing, is essential to moving up to senior positions. Sound technical knowledge without a considerable amount of savvy in this area would not be enough. Stephanie Shern commented on this matter with these words, "Your attire can make you or break you on the first contact. It affects the way your peers, people above you, and clients perceive you. I've seen women—including women who have come to work for me—walk into a room wearing completely inappropriate clothing—for example, clothes that were too casual for the circumstances or ridiculous accessories—it completely turns me off, and I know it turns off the other individuals who might be with me."[2]

The public accounting profession depends upon the client's confidence in the auditors. Without a high level of confidence, the auditor's independent review of a company's financial statements would lose credibility. For this reason and to enhance this confidence, the auditor assumes a conservative stance somewhat similar to that assumed by bankers of investment counselors. Completely out of place is the flamboyant style frequently employed by salespersons, ad agencies, or land speculators. For this reason the dress as well as the bearing of the auditor must fit the task at hand, and a professional bearing is appropriate at all times. Many college students have not yet learned to dress or act this way, and as new staff they must assimilate the necessary manners and dress so that they are natural and believable.

Until a few years ago one of the large national firms required all the men and women in the firm, from new staff to managing partners, to wear white shirts or blouses. No pastels, patterns, stripes, or checks were allowed, no matter how subtle the colors or designs may have been. Suits were the order of the day for both men and women, and they had to be conservative in color. The firm no longer enforces this type of dress code, but like all the national firms, it remains relatively conservative in its dress habits. More than one new staff member has found this constraint not to her liking, especially when she has good clothes sense and wants to be more than just another carbon copy. Nevertheless, there is a Big-Eight image and, in the words of a young staff member, their professionals are expected to have a certain *"panache."*

Local firms are not as strict as the national firms in this respect. Perhaps, because they have a closer work relationship with their clients and are personally known to them, they feel they can relax the dress code a bit.

Area Specialties

New staff members right out of college learn in just a few days, if they did not already know it, that their work for the first year or so will not be glamorous and will for the most part consist of lower-level tasks such as reviewing and checking. Perhaps this is a necessary part of learning the job, but it does become rather boring unless there is a commitment to learning what the profession is all about. The awareness that not all assignments are glamorous comes as a shock to many and can destroy the enthusiasm of those who just want a career and not a job. University programs give students a somewhat glamorous picture of the profession and, while not totally untrue, it makes a reassessment of first-year expectations necessary. This is more obvious in the audit area than in tax or consulting, for new staff are able to move more quickly into less trivial assignments in tax and consulting.

There is closer contact with corporate executives in the tax area during the first year than in other areas due to the preparation of individual tax returns and/or financial counseling. Audit and consulting have significant first year contact, but it is generally at lower levels in the organization. Here is what Norma Lauder, a tax partner in an international firm said:

> In most cases client contact increases after you are with the firm for a period of time. It obviously varies

according to client and the staffing on the job. It is, however, more likely that you will not have much client contact in the first year and that it will increase after that. It usually comes earlier with individuals rather than corporations because most corporations have a number of experienced tax personnel in-house and generally tend to want to deal with comparably experienced people. Individuals, however, generally do not have an extensive knowledge of tax law and, if the staff person is mature and gets along well with people, he or she can work with individual clients early on. Most of the work you get the first year or so with corporations is in the way of research. When I was promoted to senior I got a lot of large corporate clients with messy tax issues, and these created a kind of shock for me. Looking back on it I think there had been a tendency not to give me complex corporate problems. I had a manager who was very helpful, and I ended up doing very well.

The less complex tax assignments can be taken over almost as soon as the first training programs are completed. These first assignments are usually preparation of tax returns that are then reviewed by a more experienced person before the firm signs them, but at least the staff person has a substantive task that he or she alone is responsible for, and one that involves interfacing with the client.

Tax staff begin fairly early to do research for the more complex problems of corporate clients. They ease gradually into the tax planning aspects, for this is the more creative dimension and requires a full and complete knowledge of the tax laws and regulations.

Women on the audit staff must go to the client's place of business, and there is no way they can be hidden from the client. This is not quite so true in the tax area, because a woman can do the research and even complete a complex tax form, or undertake some of the preliminary aspects of tax planning, without ever having to be in contact with the client. There are cases in which the male members of the tax staff have the direct client contact, gather the client information, and then give it to the women members of the tax staff, who perform the work. In this way women have in effect been hidden from clients, and, needless to say, their advancement is greatly hindered.

An example of this type of discrimination recently occurred to a personal acquaintance of ours. She was working for a national firm at the time, and it left deep scars on her memory. She had a Master's degree in taxation and enough tax experience to work on complex tax problems. She transferred to another city, and in that office she was not permitted to have direct contact with clients. She was assigned one particularly complex problem, and when the smoke had cleared, there was to be a tax refund of almost a million dollars to the client. She was particularly proud of that piece of work, but when the client came into the office for the final conference she was not permitted to attend. The manager who was in charge of the meeting called her at home the night before and changed her assignments to be sure that she would be in the office that morning, "just in case I need you." They wanted to be sure that if something did come up, she would be there to handle it, but they did not want the client to know a woman had done the work. That experience was one of the reasons she left the firm a few months later to study for a Ph.D. degree and become a tax professor. She is now on the faculty teaching accounting and taxation at a well-known university. She did not want her name given here because as an accounting professor she works closely with the practicing profession and does not want to take the risk of losing their support.

In the consulting area there is less "ticking and turning" than in auditing, and less "looking up the law" than in taxation. In consulting there is always a specific problem that the client wants solved, and finding solutions to it permits more creativity, even for staff. Most of the new staff that come into this area have had specialized training, such as in computer science, production engineering, or statistics, and they sometimes have had considerable prior experience. They are assigned to consulting jobs very quickly, and there is a shorter initial indoctrination period. They are trained to interface directly with the client's management in solving the specific problem that they have been assigned. Establishing computerized systems or scientific inventory control systems are the types of problems they work on, and they may be on a single assignment for more than a year. In the first chapter of this book we briefly described the computerized system that Faith Goodland worked on at the 1984 Olympic games. This is typical of the jobs on which the consulting personnel work. The highly specialized knowledge which they must have leaves little room for "juniors," and most of them are seniors or managers almost from the time they come on board. A few staff members are needed to gather data or do the less complicated assignments, but their numbers are much fewer than in auditing or tax. Since each consulting engagement is a one-shot affair, any person in the consulting area who is good at getting new clients or new jobs is usually assured of moving on up to partner.

Although tax and consulting have their bright sides, auditing is the heart of the profession for the large national firms, and in most cases the number of new staff hired each year in the auditing area will exceed the number for both tax and consulting combined. Tax, on the other hand, is frequently the leading area in smaller local firms, and the staff working for these firms quickly find themselves having to work with taxes no matter what their preference. They must perform the audit, prepare the client's tax return, provide tax planning advice, and consult with the client in the solution of any financial or control problems that arise.

A staff accountant with a local firm in Tacoma, Washington, gave this account of her first years: "In my first three years with this firm, I worked on audit engagements of a major newspaper, a retirement community, and several federal grants. I have had responsibility for the design and implementation of manual accounting systems for a number of diverse business operations. The nature of this firm's practice also provides firsthand exposure to client services other than audit. I have performed many compilation and review engagements, as well as provided tax advice and prepared tax returns. My firm has given me the opportunity to experience all facets of client service in an effort to help me choose the service area best suited for me."

The Senior Accountant

Seniors, having several years experience as juniors under their belts, move into positions where they direct the field work of the staff. They plan the extent of the work to be done on a specific audit, the order in which the work will be carried out, and who will do the work. These matters are cleared with the manager in charge of the job, but the actual work is administered by the senior. Seniors are sometimes assigned small audits to complete themselves, with a minimum of guidance from managers. Seniors have much more meaningful client contact, and their work begins to be more personally rewarding. The manager or partner still has the final responsibility, but the actual work, carrying it all the way through until ready for final approval, is up to the senior. Seniors must make all work arrangements for the staff which have been assigned to the job, including transportation on any out-of-town assignments. They are in charge of the travel and hotel arrangements, which can sometimes be a tricky assignment. The selected hotel must not be too lavish, for the client is paying the bills, but it must not be beneath the professional status that accountants must maintain. They have secretaries and other staff persons to help with the detail of these tasks, but the arrangements are a senior's responsibility. They always have to be aware of the desires of staff members, clients, and bosses when making travel arrangements—and this is sometimes like juggling three apples at the same time. The intrinsic rewards of doing a good job are immense at this level, so that the long overtime hours are less burdensome for the senior than they are for staff persons.

Leadership Ability

Tact and gentle firmness are necessary at the senior level—more so than in most first level supervisory positions in industry. The senior is the primary contact at the client's office, and the day-to-day problems of getting the work done require not only supervision of the staff assigned to the job, but also eliciting the cooperation of the client's personnel. Clients somewhat naturally find the auditors to be a minor nuisance. Auditors are always asking questions, taking up their time, disrupting their routines, requesting documents that have to be located and replaced. The auditors must have a place to work, and this takes up office space, which is usually tight and frequently must be rearranged on a makeshift basis to accommodate the auditors. The senior will quickly find himself or herself walking a tightrope between keeping the client's personnel from being too unhappy and keeping the audit staff busy and working efficiently. The senior must see that any staff-client friction is handled quickly and effectively, and any staff member who creates an unnecessary problem must be dealt with promptly.

As a senior, a woman who is technically very qualified must now also be assertive, without being overbearing, and exhibit self-confidence and self-esteem. These personality characteristics are essential at this point in her career. Women who have not learned assertiveness and who are moved into the senior position must undergo a transition which in many cases causes enormous stress for them. They must not only assume leadership positions, directing men who may not be accustomed to women supervisors, but they must undertake this leadership position in the rather stressful surroundings of the client's office.

Promotion to senior usually requires that the individual pass the CPA exam. While not essential, this step in the career ladder is expected, and if not achieved within a reasonable period of time, the individual may be counseled to move out of public accounting. Failure to pass the exam means that the individual either does not have the technical qualifications to do so or does not have the desire. Either one is unacceptable.

One of the most frequent sayings in the profession is, "We promote our people to the next level as soon as they can handle the responsibility." Seniors are almost literally thrust into positions of heavy responsibility just as soon as they learn how to survive the "ticking and turning,"—and many cannot handle the quick movement into such a position of responsibility. Unless there is a commitment to a professional career at this point, the chances of making it to the next promotion are very slim.

Turnover

Experience as a public accountant, even at the staff level, is considered the very best training for moving into responsible positions outside of public accounting. One of the reasons for the high rate of turnover is that public accounting experience is considered by a large proportion of university students to be just a continuation of their training. The combination of a university degree, the CPA certificate, and several years of experience with a large public accounting firm qualifies individuals leaving public accounting for responsible positions in industry, and such a career path permits them to achieve these high positions in much less time than it would take if they went straight into industry. Students are aware of this as they begin their campus interviewing, and the firm's training program is a strong consideration in choosing a job upon graduation.

The turnover rate for women and men is at its peak at the senior level. When a senior decides to leave the profession, or cannot handle the job and is counseled out, the firm almost always goes out of its way to locate a suitable position in industry for the departing senior. In most cases he or she will already have located a good position with a client, especially if he or she has her certificate and has been a senior long enough to have learned how to provide leadership. Experienced seniors with CPA certificates are in high demand in industry, and they take positions of considerable responsibility when they leave the active practice of public accounting. Salaries of $40,000 to $50,000 (at 1985 salary scales) are hardly an exception for a certified senior with four or five years experience.

Industry Specialties

In the larger firms seniors and managers begin to specialize in a particular industry. Handling the assignment of individuals to jobs is a task usually controlled by the established male power structure of the firm, and there is a subtle pressure to move women toward those industries that are considered "acceptable for women." This is especially true in auditing and consulting, though not quite so noticeable in the tax area.

"Women's areas" have traditionally included the audit of banks, possibly because this was one of the first areas of commerce to have a significant number of women executives. The audit of government agencies constitutes another "woman's area," and this includes organizations such as school districts, cities and counties, and hospitals. Once an area of specialization has been selected, either overtly or more subtly, through a series of assignments, it becomes very difficult to shift to another area, although it is sometimes done.

The Manager

Managers are the persons who actually run the engagement. They supervise a number of seniors, and they have several jobs going on at the same time. One manager we talked to in Chicago said she had developed a specialty in banks; she was in charge of six banks, four holding companies, all of their subsidiaries, and a number of banks that are affiliated with out-of-state parent corporations. In addition, she was assigned a number of smaller non-bank audits.

Managers must supervise a group of seniors, and they stay in close contact with the work as it is being done, although they are not as actively or directly engaged in the actual verification work. They allocate staff and seniors to jobs, make sure the work is done on time, review the work after it has been done, settle any problems that arise during the audit, discuss the audit findings with the client, and keep the partners informed of how things are going.

Devra Shapiro, a former audit manager with a large national firm, described her daily work to us this way:

> I would say that about 50 percent of my time is spent actually managing my audits. I work with the seniors when they start the field work, reviewing their audit programs, looking at the way they have scheduled the work and have assigned staff to the audit tasks. I spend a sizeable portion of this time at the client's office staying in touch with them at the same time I am supervising the seniors. I also have to write audit reports and review audit work papers.
>
> Another 20 percent of my time is administrative. I have to evaluate the performance of my people, counsel seniors about their problems, teach them how to evaluate their staff. Then twice each year we have formal evaluation sessions where we sit down and have conferences with each senior and each staff member. I also have to plan our staffing for future jobs, and schedule work to be done. Another 20 percent is spent on special projects. There are always some special requests, either from clients or from our own office, which require my time. The remainder is spent on learning, attending training sessions, keeping up with what is new.

Managers and partners in the tax area usually handle the large corporate clients, using seniors and staff to gather the data or do the report-preparation work. The tax area is somewhat different from auditing in that there is the possibility of becoming highly specialized in a very narrow area. A tax person can specialize in international tax problems, for example. This would result in reduced client contact, because most of the work is of a research nature. But there is no way that these women specialists can be hidden from clients, for their expertise is so strong and so specialized that no one can interface with the client in their place. Sandy Norton, an international tax specialist in the Houston office of Peat, Marwick, Mitchell & Co., is an example of a highly skilled specialist. She started in the auditing area with a national firm in Pennsylvania, where she became a senior. When her husband, who was on the staff of that same firm, left to enter law school, she moved with him to Houston and joined Peat, Marwick, Mitchell & Co. in their tax area. With her husband's involvement in law school, Sandy, too, felt drawn toward law and began taking courses at night while she worked. When her husband graduated, she left work to enter law school full-time, and upon graduation returned to Peat, Marwick, Mitchell & Co. She decided at that point to specialize and began to throw all her energies toward international taxation. Today Sandy Norton is a recognized authority in that area, handling all the complex international tax problems for a large array of clients.

Evaluation Process

All of the large firms and many of the smaller ones have formal performance evaluation systems. After each job is completed, a senior is given a rating on his or her performance by the manager or partner in charge of the job, and he or she must in turn give an evaluation of each staff member that worked on the job. Male ratings for women staff, or women ratings of men, sometimes reflect a very decided bias. If a male senior consistently gives lower ratings to women staff, this fact will become apparent to the managers or partners, and this happened frequently during the first years that women were accepted in the profession. Today, since university accounting programs are almost equally divided between women and men, there is only a minimum of woman-man conflict, at least on the staff-senior-manager levels. Further, as men and women are assigned to jobs together in reasonably equal numbers, the emphasis tends to be upon performance and not gender. The biased ratings on performance are generally a thing of the past at the staff and senior level.

At the upper level, however, where the performance of managers is assessed by partners, some biases still linger. The formal ratings of managers stress elements which differ from those of seniors and staff, and managers perform functions very close to those that partners themselves perform. There are still many of the old-time male partners in the profession whose evaluations of women managers often reflect the traditional biases, and there is some evidence that many women managers are given ratings lower than men, even though their level of performance is the same. There are still many partners who have not been able to discard completely the sex-role stereotyping that leads to a belief that women are not sufficiently assertive, that they will crumble under client pressure, that clients do not like women managers as well as men managers, that women are not sufficiently committed to a lifelong career—and that most of them will probably leave shortly to have a baby. When these beliefs still exist, the performance evaluations of women will suffer, and they have to do a better job than a man just to get an equal rating. It is in the promotion of a manager to the position of partner that the effects of sex biases are still felt, and it will take a few more years before this bias dissipates.

Need for People Orientation

Skills in working with people begin to be more and more essential as the public accountant moves up the career ladder. This is true in all three areas, audit, tax, and consulting. Good technical skills are learned first at the staff level, but at the higher levels of the organization, people skills are the magic ingredient that open doors for one person and close them for another. Additional skills in working with people are necessary at the senior level, becoming progressively more important at the manager and partner levels. Some seniors have excellent technical skills, but their "people skills" are not sufficiently developed, and they must concentrate on that aspect of their work. Some seniors are able to develop these skills quickly and, of course, some never do. One woman spoke to that point in an interview with us when she said:

> Those who do not have an orientation toward people must learn it, and, if they don't, they will disappear. It

is an inherent trait, though it may not be sufficiently developed, and there are some who just don't have it and can't learn it. The best way to develop an orientation toward people is to just get out and make yourself do it. It helps a lot to be working with people who are good at it and will take time to show you how to improve. We had formal training courses at every level in the organization about how to deal with clients, how to manage our staff, how to do personnel evaluations, how to counsel people, how to terminate people. But the best learning method is on the job, and the one thing that we needed most was the efforts of those above us to help us learn how to deal with people on the job.

The Mentor

Unfortunately, teaching people how to deal with other people has been a problem as long as the human race has been on this earth. Professional people, whether they be attorneys, CPA's, corporate managers, or politicians tend to concentrate on their own tasks, and bringing others along in the organization is given a secondary priority. A real advantage accrues to an individual who has a mentor, or at least someone who will take the time to teach these very elusive interpersonal skills. Joyce Bennis, a consulting partner in the Chicago office of Arthur Young, spoke to us of the value of a mentor to her development this way:

> A mentor was extremely important in making me successful. I've had two in the course of my career here, and both of them went out of their way to make sure that I understood what was necessary to be successful. They made me able to be more successful than I could have been just based upon my skills. Both were managers, and both were men. I had no women mentors, because there weren't any women ahead of me to show me how. It will be interesting now that women are in sizeable numbers to see if they make better mentors than men. One of my two mentors was the best salesman I have ever seen. He really helped me in terms of developing an ability to understand what a client really

wanted. The other was one who was extremely good at client relations, and he could explain things to other people, such as changes that needed to be made to solve their problem, and he was incredibly successful in getting them to do it.

Joyce Bennis talked at length about these two and how they had shaped her "people orientation." She continued, "A mentor is a very personal relationship. You are a mentor because of something you get from the relationship, and you have a mentor because of something you need. It's a rich personal relationship—not something you choose, it's just something that happens." We asked her if she felt there was something in the personality of some women that kept them from accepting a mentor relationship, a stand-off attitude or a coldness. She replied, "There has to be a willingness to interact, on both sides, for the relationship to work. There is a need for humility, because you are going to find out all the things you don't know but should. You have to be open and willing to accept the things that the mentor is trying to give you. You have to hear what is being said, and they are rarely flattering. It's tough to hear, 'Boy, did you mess that up. Here is what you should have done,' or 'You shouldn't have done that. Next time do it this way.' But there is no better way to learn from your mistakes."

Age Disadvantage

The seniors and managers of CPA firms have an age disadvantage in dealing with clients. Since the career path in the larger CPA firms begins immediately after graduation from college, most new staff are only 22 or 23 years old. By the time they are 25 years old they are seniors, having contact with chief financial officers and executive officers who started their corporate experience at about the same time the seniors were born. The CPA's may still be less than 30 when they are managers, and in exceptional cases may be in their very early 30's when they are partners. Sally Meadows is one such person who commented on this, saying:

There is a certain amount of insecurity when you walk into a group of distinguished, older exectuives, and both women and men staff feel it. The people in our firm my own age have told me they feel the same thing. You just have to get to the point where you have their confidence, and all of a sudden age differences disappear. They begin to look past the young age and say, 'Well, she has the experience and she knows what she is doing' and from then on everything is equal.

Not everyone has the self-confidence to get past this hurdle, and some staff do not make the grade to senior. They may not make it because they choose not to, because they do not have the interpersonal skills, but for whatever reason, the turnover rate is highest at the senior level. The technical material which a senior must master is immense, and there is always the fear of giving bad advice, or making the wrong decision. One young practitioner expressed it this way:

Some of us get to the point where we don't even like to pick up the phone because someone's going to ask a question which we don't have the answer for. We have to steel ourselves, and not say 'I don't know.' We have to learn to say smoothly and without panic that, 'It could be this, or it could be that, and let me check to be sure what the implications are in this case.' When we learn to handle surprises in this way we begin to get comfortable with our daily work.

This takes self-confidence, interpersonal skills, technical knowledge—all the ingredients for success. New staff pick up these ingredients along the way up their career ladders, and being a partner in their own firm is the ultimate reward.

REFERENCES

1. AICPA, *The Duties of Junior and Senior Accountants,* New York, 1953, p. 1.
2. Shern, S., "A Woman CPA Looks at Public Accounting," *Management Accounting,* Vol. 61, No. 8, February, 1980, pp. 39–43.

At the Top—Big Eight Style

For decades, eight large international firms have dominated the public accounting profession. A few have altered their names, such as Haskins and Sells becoming Deloitte, Haskins & Sells, and Lybrand becoming Coopers and Lybrand. But name changes have not affected their dominance of the profession. Several other firms within the past twenty years or so have become so large that they have also entered into this elite group, so that today it is not uncommon for one to hear the phrase the "Big Nine," or the "Big Ten." All of these firms have practice offices in each of the larger cities in the U.S., and in many of the medium-sized cities also. In addition, through associated international partnerships, they have practice offices in most of the larger cities throughout the world.

These practice offices have audit, tax, and consulting activities, frequently with separate organizational units for each activity. The smaller offices may have no more than two or three partners and a dozen staff, while the largest may have up to several hundred partners and close to a thousand managers, seniors, and staff. The home offices are all in New York, with the exception of one in Chicago and another in Cleveland. Their operating policies are basically similar—including their reluctance to accept women as partners. They began hiring women staff during the late 1960's and early 1970's, but opening the firm to women as partners was slow in coming. The forces that created this resistance to admitting women to partnership have been varied, and sex biases at this level are subtle but strong. The male partners stoutly deny that a bias exists.

Early Biases

In the early days, prior to the 1960's, the partner make-up of these large international firms was purely WASP. Blacks and Jews were generally excluded from partnership, as were women. The Big Eight would hire some of these minorities as staff, but admittance to partnership was a rarity indeed. Minority groups had to form their own firms, so while a limited number did become partners, it was almost always in a local practice. A study by the U.S. Senate in 1976 revealed almost no minority group partners in the Big Eight.[1]

Big Eight firms grow in two ways. One is through hiring new staff, developing them, moving them into management positions in the firm, and eventually admitting them to partnership. The second way is through absorption of an already existing local firm into their organization. The partners in the local firm negotiate a price for their business; when an agreement is reached, they are brought into the larger firm as partners. Included in the negotiations is the decision concerning which of the local firm partners will become partners in the Big Eight firm. In this way a few minorities, including a few women, were admitted into the Big Eight as partners during the 1960's and 1970's. This was a rather rare occurrence, however, because the woman, black, or Jew, who was a local partner would usually be bought out for cash rather than be brought into the firm as a partner. Otherwise, the negotiations were never concluded and no merger occurred.

First Women Partners

The first woman partner in a Big Eight firm to reach that position by going through the ranks was Mary Jo McCann, who was made a partner in 1969. By 1977 there were eighteen women partners.[2] Most of the firms had only one or two; the largest number was four, and one of the firms had none. How many of these had become partners through the acquisition of local firms is not known.

NUMBER OF WOMEN PARTNERS IN BIG EIGHT FIRMS, 1977

Firm	No. of Partners			No. of Staff	
	Female	Male	%	Women	%
Arthur Andersen	1	720	.14	999	12.5
Arthur Young	2	544	.37	614	13.8
Coopers and Lybrand	3	599	.50	768	13.3
Ernst and Ernst	0	565	.00	800	14.7
Deloitte Haskins and Sells	1	524	.19	705	16.1
Peat, Marwick, Mitchell & Co.	4	839	.47	936	12.8
Price Waterhouse	1	417	.24	636	12.5
Touche Ross	6	692	.86	504	10.5
Total	18			5,962	

As the preceding table shows, the total number of women working for Big Eight firms in 1977 was almost 6,000, or almost 13 percent of the staff. So few women had been hired prior to 1970 that not enough time had elapsed for them to obtain sufficient experience to be admitted to partnership. This reason, which was generally given at the time, appeared plausible. The text of a New York Times article by Deborah Rankin, written September 17, 1977, is reproduced below. It gives some of the flavor of those years, and some of the existing rationale for the scarcity of women partners.

Thousands of accountants converged on Cincinnati this fall for the annual meeting of the American Institute of Certified Public Accountants, and scores among the thousands gathered at cocktail parties given by national firms in the field.

However, an informal invitation to a party for female accountants, scrawled on a piece of paper and propped up on a wash basin in the women's restroom, barely drew ten guests.

The sparse attendance reflects the progress that women have made on the conservative and overwhelmingly male profession of public accounting. In that field, as in many others, programs of affirmative action are increasing the numbers of women who are breaking the barriers.

But the greatest advances are being made in the lower echelons. The number of women who have made it to the top in accounting, like the number of women who have made it to the top in such other areas of finance as banking and insurance, is small indeed.

'Now we have members' badges instead of wives' badges,' said a female delegate to the Cincinnati meeting, in a comment on how far women have advanced in the field over the last two decades.

The Big Eight, as the largest national firms are known, have an average of 612 partners apiece, but a parallel average of 2.25 female partners. The greatest number of female partners in any one firm is six, and that firm is Touche Ross & Company, whose six partners include its comptroller.

While women make up less than 1 percent of the number of partners at Touche Ross, this showing is nonetheless twice as good, on a percentage basis, as the showings of the next most progressive firms.

One big firm, Ernst & Ernst, does not have a single female partner. When asked why the firm has not elevated one woman to a partnership, a spokesman said that Ernst and Ernst was 'waiting for the right one to come along.'

The most common explanation for the scarcity of women at the top in accounting firms is that it takes an average of twelve years for a person to rise from staff accountant to full partner, and women were not entering the profession in 1965. Why they were not is another matter.

On the one hand, the firms maintain that, in the 60's, women were not aware of the opportunities in the profession. On the other hand, women insist they were well aware of the opportunities but just couldn't get past the front door.

'None of the Big Eight would talk to me,' said one woman at the Cincinnati meeting; 'I was told they did not have space for a woman in the office.'

But things are changing dramatically. Virtually all of the major firms report that they are hiring a much larger percentage of women from college campuses than they did five years ago. At Arthur Young & Company, for instance, a spokesman said that the percentage of women recruited had grown to about 30 percent, compared with 10 percent in 1972.

After they have graduated and landed jobs with accounting firms, women generally get equal pay for equal work. But one problem of having women in managerial positions, according to Claude Rodgers, partner in charge of personnel at Arthur Andersen & Company, is that they are not assertive enough in their dealings with staff and clients.

'Sometimes you have to be tough,' Mr. Rodgers said. 'You can't continue to get angry; you have to learn how to put your foot down. When some women are faced with a difficult managerial issue,' he said, 'they try to duck it or work around it.'

'The firm,' he added, 'is trying to help women overcome their timidity by sending them to special training seminars sponsored by colleges.'[3]

The last two paragraphs of that New York Times article expresses very well the problems women had in achieving partnership in Big Eight firms. Existing partners, all male, believed that women were timid, that they ran from problems, that they were not tough enough. These same beliefs continue to be the most critical barrier to admittance of women to partnership in the Big Eight firms.

Four years later the picture had changed only slightly. *Forbes* magazine in a 1981 article revealed the promotion list of these same eight firms. It included a total of only 14 women partners, while there were 639 new male partners.[4] The earlier argument that the scarcity of women partners was due to the small number of women who had sufficient experience was beginning to lose credibility.

Profile of Women Partners

By 1983 the Big Eight firms combined had a total of only sixty-two women partners. This was only 1 percent of the total—indicating very little change in the male/female composition of partners,even though the number of women with more years of experience had increased substantially. A study of women partners in the "Big Nine" was completed by the American Women's Society of CPA's in 1983, which included these sixty-two partners from the Big Eight and seven others from another large international firm.[5]

According to this study the average age of these women partners was thirty-nine, and they had been elevated to partner at an average age of thirty-three. The majority were married (73 percent) but had no children (63 percent). They had an average college grade point overall average of 3.48 out of a perfect 4.0 and a grade point average in their accounting courses of 3.63. Some 75 percent of these women had worked while going to college. Over half of them passed the CPA exam at the first sitting, while normally only about 20 percent of the candidates, male and female, are successful the first time.

They are a very stable group. Some 73 percent of them spent their entire childhood in the same city, or moved no more than once. Approximately 80 percent graduated from the same university they had enrolled in as freshmen, and 50 percent have worked for the same firm their entire professional careers.

Supporting a New Partner

In the larger national firms a manager cannot expect to be admitted into the firm as a partner unless there are sufficient new hours of billable time to support him or her. The existing partners make their sizeable incomes by billing the time of staff, seniors, and managers to clients at an hourly rate which is considerably higher than the salaries paid. Each existing partner normally would supervise the jobs of one or two managers, who would supervise two to four seniors, and each senior may have three or more staff working for him or her. Thus each partner may have from fifteen to twenty persons working under his or her supervision. The hourly billing rate may be two or three times the individual's salary. It doesn't take much arithmetic to see that the partners do not want to water down the difference that they receive by making too many new partners.

The billing rates at the time we interviewed practicing public accountants were as follows for the tax department of one practice office of a large national firm.

Partners, per hour	$175.00
Managers, per hour	145.00
Seniors, per hour	95.00
Staff, per hour	70.00

Working 40 hours per week for 50 weeks per year, an individual can put in 2,000 hours. In public accounting there is quite a bit of nonbillable time, normally spent in training schools, recruiting, or other types of in-house activities. However, with the fairly heavy overtime which is normal in the profession, there is an expectation of something like 1500 billable hours per year. This would mean that a senior, at $95 per hour, could be expected to produce billable amounts of $142,500—and receive in salary up to $50,000. The difference, which may approach $100,000 for this one senior, is used to pay the training expenses, the office rent, supplies, recruiting costs, and similar overhead costs of the firm. These items are expensive, for the national firms go first class, but there is no doubt that a substantial part of the firm's revenues are left for partners to take home. It is natural that existing partners do not take in large numbers of new partners unless there are additional billable hours to support them.

One national firm has an unwritten policy of expecting an increase of 10,000 additional billable hours in their tax departments before a new tax partner can be admitted. This policy is obviously not written and not publicized, but managers who are approaching the point of a partnership decision are all well aware of it. They know from the amount of business done that year whether one or two tax partners can be expected, or none if business has not grown. Regardless of how competent they may be, they will not become partners unless there are additional billable hours. This policy is coupled with the usual rule-of-thumb in these large national firms that when a manager reaches the point of being ready for partnership, there can only be a wait of two to three years—if not promoted within that length of time, the individual will be counseled out of the firm.

The same general rule applies to the audit and consulting areas as for the tax area. The only way billable hours can be increased in auditing is to secure new clients, and in consulting by getting new consulting engagements. The pressure to get new clients becomes intense at the managerial level, because every manager who can sell a new company on using them as auditors can make a major step toward securing his or her own promotion to partner. A consulting contract, especially one that may take a year or so to complete and has the potential of 20,000 or so billable hours, will be in a good position to move up to the partner level. There is no denying that the most significant element in moving someone from manager to partner is the ability to secure additional work for the firm.

Actually, a great deal of luck (good and bad) accompanies the accountant as he or she progresses from staff to the point of being considered for partner. In periods of economic boom, business for accountants is good and their clients have enough financial slack to consider other than essential audit and tax services. Economic growth also creates new business, which provides new audit and tax opportunities. An economic expansion creates demand for more accountants, and thus, more partners. If a manager is being considered for partner during expansionary periods, he or she has a much higher chance of making partner than one would, with the same personal and professional qualities, during periods of economic contraction when demand for accounting services declines as a result of clients' belt-tightening. Many partners admit that at the time they came up for partner, they were in the right place at the right time.

Admitting Partners

The process of admitting new partners into a large firm is a cumbersome process, and subjective judgments must be made at several levels for each person nominated for partnership. If an existing partner is biased against any minority group or against an individual, ample opportunity exists for that bias to affect the decision.

First, the nominated person must have the expected "time in grade," which is usually from seven to twelve years, with four or five of those at the manager level. Next, he or she must be supported or "nominated" by an existing partner. One Big Eight partner explained his firm's process in this way:

Big Eight firms are usually organized by industry groups, such as Finance, or Energy, or Manufacturing. Each group has specialist partners, and a partner usually nominates some manager in his own group. One of the key elements considered is the number of partners already in that area. For example, if the firm's office in that city already has two partners in a given area, and a young manager is ready to be promoted, he or she may have to relocate because the local office does not have room for him or her there. This is not the usual case, but new partners must be ready for transfer if it is necessary. I remember one partner who was transferred to Hong Kong one week after being made partner.

The list of nominees is circulated among all partners in the firm, nationwide. Over a thousand partners receive the list. The purpose of this circulation is to determine if a partner anywhere in the firm has had an undesirable experience, either at work or of a personal nature, with the future partner. A partner in this firm may know only five percent of the people on the list, but this step safeguards against a major error occurring in accepting a partner.

The firm has a regional partner in charge of a region which may cover several states. This regional partner reviews the list and he usually knows most of the people on it personally, especially those in his region. He unilaterally can make eliminations and deferrals to next year. Deferrals occur because some individuals may need to wait a year, or perhaps two, and when this happens the individual is personally counseled. The purpose of the regional partner's review is to maintain balance in the number of partners within the firm's offices, within regions, and within specialty areas. This step gets the list into shape for presentation to the firm's national group, called the Board of Directors.

The final step in the process is approval by the Board, which is composed of a dozen or so of the firm's senior partners. The list they see is the final one, and they review it for consistency and equity, and to be sure that the firm's standards are maintained.

As is evident by this process, if a regional partner or member of the board had a personal bias, it would undoubtedly affect his decision, and a person or a group of persons could be held back. A powerful force which tends to hold women back in the Big Eight is the conservative stance which predominates thoughout, making an existing male partner hesitant to nominate a woman manager in his specialty area until she has proved herself far more than a male would have to. No existing partner wants to look bad with a nomination that is struck down at a higher level. The "being tough" syndrome is strong. An existing partner holds back a nomination of a woman unless she is "tough" enough, but he will also hold her back if she is "overly aggressive" or "comes on too strong." Few of us, men or women, can convince every member of a large group that we are neither of these. As a result, women partners in the Big Eight are indeed scarce.

Another Big Eight firm, in its promotion process, requires that a nomination be screened first by all the partners in the nominee's local office and then by the managing partner of that office. The nominations that survive this process go to the national office, where another screening group approves the nominee. Those remaining are submitted to all partners throughout the firm for approval. Actual "yes" and "no" votes are taken on each nominee, and several thousand partners will cast a vote on each nominee. A 95 percent "yes" vote is necessary for the nominee to be accepted into the partnership. Each nominee must sign an agreement that he or she will accept the responsibilities of partnership, if elected, and be willing to relocate if it is required.

The screening process includes consideration of a number of personal and performance characteristics. The following list is used by one Big Eight firm and, as is evident, there is little about the individual's person or performance that is not considered.

QUALIFICATIONS TO BE CONSIDERED FOR PERSONS NOMINATED FOR PARTNERSHIP

* Professional Competence
  Application of technical knowledge
  Current technically
  Judgment (when to decide and when to consult)
  Engagement planning, supervision, and control

* Client Service
  Client confidence and satisfaction with professional service and advice
  Contacts with chief executives, audit committees, and board members
  Responsiveness

* Practice Development
  Initiative, innovation and imagination
  Synergism with other departments
  New work with present clients
  New clients obtained
  General promotion of Firm (articles, speeches, etc.)
  Participation in professional and community activities
* Leadership and Personnel Development
  Subordinate's confidence
  Accessibility and availability to subordinates
  Recruitment and development of staff
  Leadership of staff on engagements and in other areas (practice development, community activity)

* Management and Administration
  Ability to get things done
  Billing and collections
  General administration
  Profit contribution

* General and Personal
  Self-motivation (initiative, drive, energy)
  Cooperation and team play
  Personal strength (courage to meet opposition)
  Peer values (how other partners regard you)
  Poise and social conduct
  Commitment to Firm and scope of interest
  Participation in professional development programs

Evaluation of Partners

A partner's share of the firm's profits is determined by the number of "units" or "shares" which he or she has. The number of units is determined by the relative contribution each partner makes to the firm, which is a complex process. In some firms the partners prepare annual evaluations of themselves, indicating everything they have done during the year and how they perceive their contribution to the firm. A partner may also prepare an evaluation of another partner in that office, if he or she wishes to do so. This happens only when a partner has been exceptionally bad or exceptionally good, and the partner doing the evaluation wishes to call attention to this fact. These evaluations go to the managing partner of that local office. The managing partner then evaluates each partner in that practice office, inserting into the process his or her own personal views. These final evaluations go to the national office, and each partner's "units" are determined for the year.

Annual evaluations of partners are similar in nature to the subjective judgments necessary in the decision to admit a new partner. One firm requires that each partner evaluate himself or herself on a forced 100 point basis, with 20 points allotted to each of five different categories. Thus each partner reports a grade of 73, or 85, or some similar numerical score, similar to a score given on a classroom test.

Still another Big Eight firm utilizes an extensive checklist with evaluative comments in its process of measuring each partner's contributions. The checklist contains over forty separate areas to be evaluated, including the following categories:

* Personal competence in the area of specialization
* Personal qualities
* Effectiveness in client services
* Effectiveness in accomplishing annual objectives
* Entrepreneurial skills
* Growth potential

Women Managing Partners

The strong role played by the managing partner of a practice office is very evident. Few women have been named to managing partner positions in the Big Eight, perhaps because there are so few women partners, and most of them have been made partner only within the past few years. More likely, the small number of women managing partners is due to the traditional resistance to women in leadership positions.

The first national firm to name a woman partner to the managing position was Laventhol and Horwath. In 1982 this firm, slightly smaller than any of the Big Eight, had 271 partners nationwide. Carol Birkholz was named that year to manage its Seattle practice office.[6] She is quoted in the newsletter of the AICPA as saying: "It's just part of the numbers game. When the profession is hiring 50 percent women, eventually they will get into positions like managing partner."

Perhaps she is right. Now that the profession is hiring 50 percent women, it may just be a matter of time, assuming there is no bias against women managers! At least in her case the bias was not sufficient to prevent her appointment to managing partner—but at this point she has been the only one in a national firm.

Firing of Partners

Difficult as it is to make partner in a large international firm, firing a partner is even more difficult. In most national firms a very high percentage of the firm's governing board, usually 90 to 95 percent, must approve the action. It is a rare occasion when this happens, primarily because extremely heavy peer pressures are utilized as the severing mechanism, and these pressures are brought to bear before a case reaches the governing board. Price Waterhouse, one of the oldest and most conservative of the Big Eight, has had only one partner in its entire history who held on until board action removed him from the firm.[7]

Continuing Biases

The conservative stance of the large accounting firms has produced a conservative approach to the acceptance of women as partners. One of two primary arguments presented in defense of this reluctance, and one that was alluded to earlier in this book, is that women may not be "tough" enough when they encounter client resistance to something which must be done in order to "certify" the financial statements. Existing male partners feel that the woman may give in to this pressure and permit the release of incorrect financial statements, thereby opening up the potential for an expensive legal suit against the auditors. Such suits have increased substantially in recent years because of a general tendency in our society to look for a scapegoat when something goes wrong. Other professions, especially the legal and medical, have experienced similar increases in the suits brought for malpractice and negligence. Public accounting firms are not exempt from this public liability, and multi-million dollar suits occur each year, brought by some stockholder who has lost money and blames the loss on an auditor's error or negligence. Not being "tough" enough is not an idle concern, but it is one that can easily be overdone and can be used as an excuse if personal biases exist.

The second of the avowed reasons for not accepting women as readily as men is that women are not good at "practice development." This is the term used in the profession for getting new business, locating new clients, and increasing the billable hours. Partners in large firms spend as much time on this aspect of their work as they do in completing audits or giving consulting or tax advice. Some of their best and most productive work in the practice development area occurs at the country club, at cocktail parties, and other places frequented by prospective controllers, treasurers, and corporate presidents. These corporate executives are the ones who select auditors and contract for consultants, so wherever they are is where the partner needs to be, selling the firm, being visible, gaining the confidence and respect of the executive.

The disadvantage which women have in selling new work to potential clients is not a small one. The sex-role stereotyping existing today which says that men should be the auditors, consultants, and tax advisors makes men reluctant to bare their financial souls to women. Business clubs, private restaurants, and civic organizations which forbid women membership have added to the difficulty of selling to corporate executives the services which public accountants offer. The social behavior patterns which make it difficult for women to invite men to lunch or dinner, or for a weekend fishing or hunting trip, all work to the disadvantage of women in securing new clients.

The smaller, local firms present somewhat the same problem for women, though considerably reduced. The clientele of these firms is usually smaller businesses, with more personal contact, where women can interface with potential clients more easily. Potential clients who are owners of small-to-medium-sized businesses may be contacted on a more personal basis, and for the local practitioner, the exclusive clubs and organizations used by top executives of the large Fortune 500 companies are not where business contacts are made.

Male partners claim that because of traditional or expected social behavior, women cannot perform as well as men in this type of business contact. Men also resist playing golf and tennis with women who are not exceptionally good.

Like the "tough" issue, the practice development dimension can also be used as an excuse in order to cover up underlying biases. The few women partners that do exist in the Big Eight are proving that practice development is not solely a man's prerogative.

Profile of a Woman Partner

Carol McElyea is an example of how a woman partner can successfully blend managerial expertise, technical accounting expertise, and practice development, as a Big Eight partner must. She is currently a partner with the Chicago office of Touche Ross & Co. in their management consulting division. She joined the firm in 1975 after spending five years with Ford Motor Company as a financial analyst, and was made a partner in 1981.

Carol grew up in a small Missouri town sixty miles from St. Louis, where her father, mother, brother, and sisters, grandparents, uncles, and aunts all lived and worked as a close-knit family group. She attended a small high school, where she was a strong student, but she said she "was not a strong competitor for the school valedictorian the year I graduated." Carol McElyea was in the school band, lettered in volleyball and track, and joined every organization in the school in which she had even the slightest interest. The people-orientation skills which enabled her to achieve partnership in the Big Eight were evident even then.

After graduation from high school she enrolled in Wheaton College, an all-women's school in Massachusetts with an enrollment of 1,200 very sharp young women. She started out as a math major, but found math too theoretical and impractical. Early in her college career Carol McElyea took a course in economics. "I fell in love with it," she said, "and continued to take a very heavy mathematically-oriented economics program. I enjoyed econometrics and model building, and I was granted a National Science Foundation Fellowship during my junior year. I ended up writing a thesis, which was not required, and graduated Cum Laude."

After graduation her appetite for more knowledge in her chosen area prompted Carol McElyea to enroll in an MBA program at the University of Missouri. She graduated with honors and a straight A average, even though she was working with Ford Motor Company as an analyst and able to take only a part-time course load. Ford transferred her to the Detroit division in 1972, where she obtained experience in the financial aspects of the business and became familiar with the political and behavioral processes that exist in large organizations. While her experiences there were invaluable, her curiosity pushed her onward. "I left Ford for several reasons," Carol McElyea said, "although my experiences there were very good for me. It was an extremely structured environment, and I wanted more diversity. That's why I was looking toward the management consulting environment. If I had stayed at Ford, I would have spent the rest of my life with the automotive industry and I wanted to see more of the world than that."

When she joined the Chicago office of Touche Ross & Co. there were two women already in the consulting division of that office. She was immediately placed on a very extensive consulting engagement that occupied her for over a year. As the only woman on that team Carol McElyea faced some of the problems of breaking new ground, and her Ford Company experience came in handy. "I was accustomed from Ford to being the only woman in an environment, and it did not bother me. At Ford I was the only woman allowed in the assembly plant and the only woman in the corporate analysis office. I had a great deal of scar tissue in terms of being the only woman. Ford has changed since then, but changes in heavy industry like that have come slower than in areas like accounting."

As a consulting partner Carol McElyea must be heavily involved in client contact, not only in completing consulting contracts, but in selling new engagements. Approximately half of her time is spent in meetings with clients, working on client engagements, interviewing people, and explaining her recommendations to clients. Another 30 percent is spent in selling, primarily in gathering data and preparing proposals, presenting the proposals to prospective clients, and convincing prospective clients that Touche Ross is the right firm to do the job. The remaining 20 percent of her time is spent in building her staff, in administrative work, and in her own professional training. Her area of expertise, or the special skills she brings to clients, is in the area of financial management, management control systems, organization structures, and fitting data processing systems into the management environment.

She discounts almost entirely the proposition advocated by many male partners that a woman would be at a disadvantage in selling professional business consulting. Glancing at the set of golf clubs nestled in a corner of her office, she commented on the fact that selling a business consulting expertise is not like selling a product like a vacuum cleaner. "We do a great deal of recurring work. When clients think we have done a good job, they will call us when they have another problem to solve. A great deal of our practice development consists of maintaining good client relationships after a job is completed. Golf, tennis, lunches are the way we stay in contact so that when they think of a consultant, they think of us first. Yesterday I was with a client that we have not had a consulting contract with for three years, but we must continue to stay in contact if we want to have a competitive edge."

Her husband, an attorney, is well aware of the need for her to stay in contact with her clients. He is supportive, according to Carol McElyea, and he knows that support is essential in a marriage where both partners are professional persons. "I can't imagine a successful marriage in a professional world without a supportive spouse," she said, "and I don't view the need for support any differently for a male than for a female. I am supportive of his work, and it's a two-way street."

She has a three-year-old boy and agrees that children place additional constraints on a professional career. "Children make one more jealous of the time they have at home, and I am less enthusiastic about a consulting contract with an out-of-town client that will take months to complete. As a partner in the firm I have more control over that type of assignment, and I can fly home every few days."

When asked what there is about management consulting that gave her the greatest satisfaction, her enthusiasm, energy, and strong intellectual curiosity came through clearly. "We really don't succeed at anything unless we have fun doing it. The bottom line is that I thoroughly enjoy what I do. What makes it fun? The feeling of achievement, of seeing something you have built grow, be implemented, and strengthen the client where a weakness once existed. I get satisfaction from hiring new staff and watching them grow and develop into first-class consultants. Finally, being able to learn from one consulting job and use that experience to help someone else gives me a great deal of satisfaction. I don't think there is much about my career that I would change."

REFERENCES

1. *The Accounting Establishment, A Staff Study,* The Subcommittee on Reports, Accounting, and Management of the Committee on Government Operations, U.S. Senate, 94th Congress, 2nd Session, December, 1976, pp. 845–871.
2. Rankin, Deborah, "More Women Moving Into Public Accounting, but Few to Top," *The New York Times,* Saturday, September 17, 1977, p. 183.
3. Ibid.
4. "Ms. CPA," *Forbes,* August 17, 1981, p. 8.
5. From a press release given out by Judi Schindler of the AWSCPA, dated June 10, 1983.
6. *Public Accounting Report,* AICPA, Vol. 5, No. 3, March, 1982, p. 7.
7. Stevens, Mark, *The Big Eight,* Collier Books, New York, 1981, p. 25.

Women Partners in Local Firms

Local practitioners are the heart of the profession. There are more CPA's in local practice than there are in the large international firms, and this is especially true of women CPA's. Prior to the last decade, when women were not accepted in the large firms, they had little choice other than to work with local firms accepting small- and medium-sized businesses as their primary clientele. In some cases these local CPA firms were established with a single CPA as the owner, while in others two or more operated as partners. Regardless of the partnership makeup, these women were in a position to concentrate on whatever aspect of the profession was of interest to them, whether it be auditing, tax, or consulting, and to develop whatever type of clientele they wished.

Rewards of Local Practices

Two rewards come from owning one's own firm that make such an arrangement the dream of almost every professional woman, whether she is an attorney, CPA, physician, or licensed engineer. The first of these is being one's own boss—not having to answer to someone else's wishes, and being able to chart one's own course. Freedom of choice and action is another way of describing this aspect of being self-employed.

The second desirable aspect of being in business for one's self is the pride of ownership and the knowledge that any success accruing to the business is due to one's own efforts. Watching the business grow and prosper and being able to develop employees from inexperienced staff to seasoned professionals can be an exhilarating experience. In smaller, local CPA firms there is the added satisfaction of being personally close to both employees and clients. This element of satisfaction is very important.

Annette Brenner and Judith Pizzica, partners in their own local firm in Philadelphia, stated that the one unexpected benefit to them when they started their firm was the tremendous high one gets from being the boss. They said:

> Selling our services to a prospective client is like selling ourselves. The rush of elation and pride that comes with a client saying, 'We'd like to use you' can smooth out many a bad day. Being the boss is a new experience for most women. Traditional women's roles have always been of the supportive nature—wife, nurse, secretary. We have chosen a career that society values. Each project undertaken generates external reinforcement of our feelings of accomplishment and self-worth. We are in control of our lives.
>
> Of course, everything has a price tag and some responsibilities never change. We pay for our "high" by stealing time from other areas of our lives. Dining out replaces entertaining at home. Novels are put aside for professional journals, and an open house at school means working instead of an evening of TV. We walk a tightrope, trying to balance the firm, marriage, children, and a personal life. With vital support from our husbands, we believe we have succeeded in keeping that balance.[1]

Single Proprietorship vs. Partnership

There are advantages and disadvantages to both the single proprietorship and the partnership. When one operates as the sole owner, she has complete control of the firm and can do whatever she deems appropriate. However, she does not have another partner to help on difficult problems nor to assist when there is more to do than she can handle herself. On the other hand, when a partnership exists there is the problem of getting along with each other. Annette and Judith expressed their views on such personal conflicts in this way:

> The first year of any partnership is the time to resolve conflicts and problems. The fact that we were not personal friends before starting the firm was a benefit. Nothing could be assumed about likes and dislikes, making open, honest discussions easier as well as necessary. The discovery that our personal ethics and work habits were similar proved to be a bonus.
>
> We have come to realize that our major problems of fees, collections, timeliness of work, and practice development are common to all CPA firms. It is 'minding our store' effectively that puts the largest demands on us. Our interests have broadened from simply doing the accounting work, to managing our own business. To achieve this we attempt to have weekly partners' meetings to discuss accounts, work in progress, accounts receivable, personnel, and any problems.

There are some aspects of operating a small firm that present greater problems than would exist in larger firms, primarily the area of staff recruiting, staff training, and keeping up with the constant stream of new knowledge which the professional must have at her fingertips. The larger firms have specialized staff training personnel and facilities, are able to send batteries of recruiters to campuses, and have specialists in almost every area of the profession. These economies of scale work to the advantage of the larger firms, but this is one of the prices that the local practitioner must pay in order to receive the added satisfaction of private ownership, freedom of choice, and close personal relationships with clients and employees.

A partner in a local firm located in San Francisco expressed these sentiments this way: "My first job after graduating from college was with a national CPA firm. I learned a great deal about auditing but did not feel I was given enough exposure to tax or management services work. I have been with a local firm for five years now and have never enjoyed my work more."

"In addition to management responsibilities, I'm involved with auditing, consultation on financial matters, and some tax work. My contacts are with the presidents, financial officers, and owners of the medium and small businesses we serve. My exposure to different industries and types of businesses has given me an in-depth knowledge of how businesses operate."

Another partner in a local firm in Madison, Wisconsin, stated, "Two of my partners and I left a large firm five years ago to start this practice. We went into debt to do it. We had two goals: to provide quality accounting service to the community and to be our own bosses. Today we employ forty people. Like most local practitioners I know, we're entrepreneurs. It's been thoroughly rewarding—and fun—to build this practice from scratch."

Starting a Local Practice

It is interesting to note that both of the partners quoted above left one firm to start their own. This is not an unusual pattern, since several years of experience are required before a state license to practice can be issued. This dictates that the CPA must practice somewhere prior to hanging out his or her own shingle. The tens of thousands of women who have been hired by both local and national firms since the late 1970's are now reaching a point in their careers where starting their own firm is a viable option. Linda Canney, a partner in a local CPA firm in Seattle and president of the American Society of Women Accountants in 1978, expressed the view several years ago that more and more women are starting to think about owning their own firms. She cited increased attendance at management seminars as indicative that women are becoming more interested in forming their own partnerships.[2] She said, "Five years ago only twenty or thirty women were coming to these seminars. Last year there were one hundred and this year over five hundred."

The experience of Annette Brenner and Judith Pizzica is somewhat typical of how a firm gets started. Annette graduated from college before accounting firms were hiring women, and some refused even to interview her. She was persistent, however, and eventually took a job with a small national firm and became certified. She left that firm when her husband was transferred and joined a small firm in another city doing "write-up work." Suddenly widowed and with a small son, she was needed to return to a position that was more financialy rewarding and eventually wound up in the tax department of a large firm. Wanting to be her own boss, the possibility of starting her own firm became one of her considerations.

Her eventual partner, Judith Pizzica, graduated from a women's college, where she was taught that a woman could be whatever she wanted to be. She learned there were constraints, however, when accounting firms were obviously reluctant to accept her. She went to work for a small firm to get the necessary experience, doing menial assignments, she left as soon as she had sufficient experience to sit for the CPA exam, and upon returning to a larger city found a large accounting firm which hired her and gave her more substantive assignments. She left that position to start her family but continued to work part-time for a small local CPA firm while three children were born and reached school age. She then felt ready to begin the partnership and move into more challenging professional work.

At this point Annette Brennan and Judith Pizzica, attending a meeting of the American Society of Women Accountants, began a conversation that included the advantages and joys of being in practice for one's self. Both had considered the possibility as attractive, and their conversation began to plant seeds. They were sufficiently serious about the possibilities of forming a partnership that they discussed the subject further over a long lunch—determined that it could and should be done.

Once they decided to become partners, their early decisions centered around the philosophy of the firm, since both were committed to quality work regardless of the fee. They were aware of the importance of the personal touch and the necessity of being available to clients. They established very early on the practice of keeping each other informed about whatever client work was in progress. Though one assumed the position of account administrator for each client, the other partner was included and was able to answer questions should the account administrator be unavailable. They were true partners, not just two people operating under a single firm name. Personal contact and attention became their strong selling points. Their clients, naturally, appreciated such personal service.

The women who start their own practices usually came from one of two positions—either they have left full-time practice to start their own firm, beginning with part-time commitments, or they are currently employed by a firm which they leave to start their own. In either case, the two critical problems are obtaining sufficient investment to get the firm underway, and getting enough clients to keep the firm alive and growing. The required investment includes more than just the cost of office furniture, or a few months' rent for an office. The biggest share of the investment covers the absence of a salary for months. It may take a year or more to generate sufficient income to cover all expenses.

Office equipment costs can be substantial for a fully equipped professional office. Desks, file cabinets, lamps, and items of this kind can absorb a sizeable amount of capital, and many persons find that working out of the home is the best way to cut costs. After becoming established, the new partners move to an office location. A computer of some kind is practically a necessity today, and its cost is dropping so rapidly that this item is no longer the heavy burden it once was. The library of a public accountant can be an expensive capital outlay, and access to a full tax library is essential. Some beginning accountants make use of the tax materials available in public libraries, which in some of the larger cities are reasonably complete. Eventually, however, a library must be purchased, if only for the sake of convenience.

Obtaining Clients

Acquiring clients is the greatest problem facing any new professional who opens an office. Fortunately for public accountants, their clients provide a great deal of repeat business, for audits are performed annually, as well as the provision of tax advice or the preparation of tax forms. However, the initial acquisition of enough clients to make the business a success is not always easy. Women have a more difficult job in this area, since they encounter social barriers in meeting prospective clients. They normally are not as free as men to join and circulate at country clubs, on the golf courses, or at civic club meetings such as the Rotary Club, Lions, or Jaycees (Junior Chamber of Comerce). A 1984 Supreme Court decision prohibits the exclusion of women from membership in civic clubs; the social taboos that once prohibited the freedom of women to move in these circles are rapidly disappearing.

Adherence to good business practices is always the best way to secure new clients, and the need to find and keep good clients usually causes women to be more conscientious about exercising good practices. One woman partnership reported that they secured a valuable client because they returned his phone call promptly. His former accountant had waited days to return his calls. This same firm secured several new clients when they held an open house to show off their new offices and invited all their friends, business contacts, and people in neighboring offices to attend.

When a CPA leaves one firm to start his or her own business, frequently a few select clients leave the old firm and go to the new one. This provides an income base that is invaluable. Many CPA's, both women and men, who start their own firms, lure a few choice clients to go with them. At first glance this may seem unethical, but it is one of the facts of professional life. The rules of professional conduct and ethics indicate that a CPA who takes a client away from another should contact the former CPA to discuss the matter, but there is nothing to prevent a client from changing accountants. There are innumerable cases where a senior or manager who is certified, but not a partner, wishes to leave the firm he or she is working for and knows a few top clients who will bring their business to the new firm. If it is discussed with the employing firm, then all the ethical requirements have been met. The employers can make that senior or manager a partner if they do not wish to lose the clients, or they can offer some other incentive to stay. They can talk to the clients and try to prevent them from changing. However, if the clients want to go to the new firm, there is no way to stop them from going.

When a CPA becomes senior or manager, having primary responsibility for clients, he or she is in a position to start thinking about the possibility of starting his or her own firm. Clients, who have gained confidence in a CPA's work, become more attached to the person professionally than to the firm itself. After all, he or she is the one doing the work, and if he or she starts his or her own firm, it makes little difference to the client what the title or address of the firm is—they want an individual in whom they can have confidence doing the work. So, if a CPA leaves the present firm and starts his or her own, the clients will follow. The same is true of attorneys, physicians, and other professionals. The one difference between the CPA and most other professionals is that only two or three major clients are needed to provide a sufficient base to support the new firm.

We interviewed two young women who had recently started their own firm, and the experiences which led to that decision are repeated almost every day in public accounting. They had worked together in the office of a large national firm for a number of years, both reaching the level of manager. When they started their own business, a few clients requiring heavy tax work went with them from the national firm, providing a sound base of clients right from the start. Within a few years they had built an excellent local tax practice.

The father of one of the young women is a physics professor, and she has a degree in math. She went on to pursue a Master's degree in accounting, specializing in tax, and graduated in the late 1970's when the national firms were hiring large numbers of women. Her background and capabilities made her a prime candidate, and she had her choice of firms. She stayed with the firm she selected for seven years before forming her own partnership.

The other young CPA also majored in mathematics but changed to accounting before graduating. The tax area was of interest to her because it placed her closer to the individual client more quickly than did auditing or consulting. She joined the large national firm at the same time as her future partner, and they became good friends as well as business associates. Specializing in oil and gas taxation and real estate taxation, she was very quickly given sole client responsibility and the authority to sign complicated tax returns in the firm's name after only four and one-half years' experience.

When with the large national firm, they had both worked primarily with closely held companies, where the owner was also president or chairman of the board. Their contacts were directly with these top people, and to these individuals the women were the firm, even though they were not partners of it. When they started their own firm, many of these clients naturally followed them. Their client base is now almost exclusively corporations and partnerships, a great many of which are in the oil and gas industry, which has unusually complex tax problems. Needless to say, they are well rewarded for their efforts, and they both are emphatic about the rewards of being one's own boss.

When they discussed their leaving the national firm for

which they were working, they were surprised that there was only a minimum degree of anger or recrimination. The partners of large national firms for the most part are sympathetic to managers who leave to embark on new careers, whether it be an employee of a client or as a partner in their own firm. The firm they left was disappointed, of course, but the parting was amicable. One of the Houston offices of another large national firm has an "alumni" association for former employees, with occasional meetings and a regular newsletter. Ex-public accountants can be very loyal to their former firms when they know that the firm has acted in the best interests of the departing individual.

However, the *partners* of an existing firm may not leave their current partners to start their own firm and take existing clients with them. This would be equivalent to unilaterally dissolving the existing partnership. Most partnership agreements have specific covenants that prohibit such actions. Managers, however, do not have such covenants and are free to leave, just as is any other employee.

When asked what type of personality a woman must have to leave the security of one firm to start her own, one woman who has done so said:

> It would have to be an aggressive person, and one not afraid to take a risk. While we did not think about it at the time, I suppose we were a bit more risk-oriented than some of the others. They are more ambitious and more goal oriented, also, and are willing to put in the hours it takes to make it to the top.

Client Make-Up

Local practitioners generally serve only small- and medium-sized businesses. An audit of a large business with thousands of employees will normally require a sizeable battery of auditors at certain points in the examination, if for only a few days. A smaller firm cannot afford to have this many people on the payroll unless there are other large clients to which these employees can be assigned as they complete a job. Thus it is usually true that large businesses must utilize large accounting firms. When the business is large enough to have branches or divisions scattered around the country, there is no other way to complete an audit except to assign a large number of auditors to the task, and a smaller local firm does not have the personnel to handle that kind of client.

Local and regional CPA firms usually have clients located near their offices, and a local practitioner usually does not have to travel on overnight assignments nearly as much as his or her counterpart in a large national firm. Consequently, much closer working relationship is developed with the clients. He or she becomes not just an auditor, or a tax specialist, but a business advisor capable of giving help on a host of problems. Financing the business is one area in which clients frequently need help. Working with bankers, attorneys, and other finance people is a regularly encountered task. Assistance in compliance with a maze of governmental regulations is another area in which the auditor frequently provides a much needed service. Such governmental organizations as the Securities and Exchange Commission, Internal Revenue Service, Federal Trade Commission, Interstate Commerce Commission, and similar agencies have introduced a complex set of rules and regulations that bewilder many managers. These regulations are often inconsistent and even directly conflicting. Without professionals such as CPA's to provide assistance, many small- and medium-sized businesses would be in serious trouble.

Sources of Clients

Women who are in practice for themselves attract a large number of women clients. Finance was one of the first areas of business to accept women, and women CPA's find that other women in the world of finance are their best clients and their best source of other clients. Burroughs Clearing House in 1979 released a report which described financial institutions as being in the forefront in naming women to their boards of directors.[3] They reported that 64 percent of the financial institutions have women directors, as compared to an overall 28 percent, which included industrial and retail companies throughout the country. The increased presence of women on boards of directors appears to be part of the new "age of accountability" which has produced increased participation by segments of our society that before have been unrepresented.

These women board members have a vote on who the company's auditors will be, and there is evidence that they are not on the boards for cosmetic purposes. They are there because they have proved themselves in the business community, and most of them have extensive business experience. The American Institute of CPA's appointed Barbara Franklin to its Board several years ago. She is not a practicing CPA, but does have heavy managerial experience at Singer and at the C. T. Bank. She also has expertise in government circles, having served as a presidential assistant to President Nixon. In that governmental assignment she started the first White House program to recruit women for high federal posts.

Banking, as the leading activity within the financial world, is experiencing an exceptionally high growth rate in the number of women officers and managers. This has direct implications for women CPA's, because these women bank officers and managers are in positions that permit them to recommend a CPA firm to their clients when they need one. More than 31 percent of all bank officers and managers are women,[4] and this proportion is growing.

California appears to be a leader in accepting women in banking. Again, Burroughs Clearing House reported that there are a number of banks there backed by and operated primarily for women.[5] Several have placed the word "woman" or "women" in the corporate title, including *The Woman's Bank* in San Diego, the *Western Women's Bank* in San Francisco, and *First Women's Bank of California* in Los Angeles. They are operated and managed almost exclusively by women for mostly women customers.

CPA's and financial executives work closely with each other. Because of the subtle pressures that continue to be exerted on women in both accounting and high finance, they have more than the normal amount of empathy for one another's problems. Many of the local chapters of CPA's devote one of their monthly meetings to a joint meeting with the local group of bank executives to discuss their common interests. This type of association provides local women CPA's with the opportunity to get to know bankers, especially other women bank executives; from this source come many of their clients.

Businesses that need financing (this includes almost all of them at one time or another), come to banks with requests for loans or extensions of credit. The bank officer cannot make a sound decision on these requests unless there is information concerning the financial affairs of the business. At this point, the CPA enters the picture because he or she has the expertise to express an opinion on the financial affairs of the business. Thus bankers and CPA's share a vital and mutual interest.

Most commercial loan executives regularly request an independent audit before granting a loan of any size to a business, especially if the business is new or increasing the size of its loan requests. Most CPA's cultivate friendships with bank executives, particularly in the years preceding the formation of their own businesses.

There are many other sources of business for the newly-formed firm. Many women CPA's have developed extensive practices from an almost entirely female clientele. One woman partner said, "We probably have a higher percentage of female clients than other accounting firms. Most of them are widows in need of estate work, and women in the process of divorce, though we do some female-owned corporation work. Why did these women hire a woman CPA? Many tell us they feel more comfortable with us and appreciate our interest in their progress and problems. Is this more than just personality? Perhaps. Perhaps not."[6]

Male clients of women CPA's are rarely sexist. That kind of client would avoid choosing a woman professional of any type, especially one to give him financial advice. Most women CPA's welcome men clients, because their businesses are usually larger and more established companies. When her firm performs work that is truly professional, and the client is a fairly large local business, the resulting word-of-mouth advertising is the best way to build a solid clientele.

Problems in Local Practice

As the firm grows, so does the number of problems that must be resolved. Staffing is perhaps the greatest of these, since good, dependable staff members are difficult to find in any area of business, and public accounting is no exception. Women tend to have greater empathy for other women who want a professional career in public accounting, and for this reason women partners tend to hire a large portion of women to fill their new staff positions.

Smaller firms have a more difficult time recruiting than the larger firms, for a number of reasons. University faculty biases toward the larger national firms is perhaps the greatest, and professors tend to steer the best graduates toward these. Possession of a full-time recruiting staff is another reason the large firms have an advantage, because they are able to concentrate on recruiting year round. Smaller local firms, including women-owned firms, must spend a proportionally greater amount of time to find the one or two good new staff members that they need each year.

Staff training also presents a problem for smaller firms, because they do not have a sufficient number of new staff members to have organized in-house training programs. They must rely upon training courses offered by state societies or the AICPA, which are not always exactly what is needed. Each firm has its own individual training needs caused by the differences in its internal policies, the makeup of its clients, the industry in which it specializes, and whether it emphasizes audit, tax, or consulting. Many of the local firms have banded together to provide a group training arrangement, utilizing regional or national joint training programs.

Constant updating is as necessary in public accounting as it is for a physician, and perhaps more so than for an attorney. There are constant changes in the tax laws, in the mass of governmental regulations, and in the auditing standards and accounting procedures that govern the CPA's daily work. The constant need to stay up-to-date has produced in almost every state a requirement that every CPA engage in a minimum number of training hours each year. This is expensive and time-consuming, but it does insure better service by every member of the profession.

Women's Professional Absences

A significant number of women withdraw from active participation in the profession for family reasons. The desire to do so is a natural extension of a woman's biological make-up. Even those who do not leave and stay with the profession all their lives have to consider seriously the impact of choosing to remain single or childless. Margaret Henning and Ann Jardin interviewed forty-five senior women executives in a company they were studying and found without exception that these top women considered interrupting their careers to pursue the human relationship of marriage and family by the time they reached the middle management level.[7] We found this innate desire in the women CPA's that we interviewed, almost without exception. The length of time they had been in the profession made little difference in the fact that family considerations had been a serious concern at some point in their lives. The sad fact is that public accounting has not yet geared itself for readmitting those who leave the profession for a while.

We found in our interviews a number of women who started their own firms as a result of leaving active practice for a while and then finding that reentry to an established firm presented a problem. The large national firms have resisted taking a woman back into their organizations after she had been out for a period of time, unless she had some special training or expertise that they needed. Career ladders within large firms are rigid, and the reentry of women remains a problem, although many of these firms are aware that this is a problem that needs to be addressed.

Reentry into local firms is a bit easier than into larger national firms, perhaps due to the disadvantage that smaller firms have in recruiting at the university level, and perhaps because the career path in these firms is not so rigid. Many women who have families are able to reenter on a part-time basis, helping out during the tax season, or assisting on major audits or consulting engagements. Frequently these women, not working full time, are able to pick up a few clients of their own at the same time, and slowly begins to build their own practice. This has been the traditional way in which women have built up practices while maintaining their families. As far back as 1963 Miona Hoffman wrote in *The National Public Accountant:*

> There are opportunities for qualified accountants, especially women, to conduct tax-related and other accounting services from their homes during the years when they have small children who need their attention. Doctors, dentists, and small businesses need this service because they do not require full-time accounting personnel. Accounting, being primarily a mental process, does not require large amounts of space or equipment. And government provides tax relief for the part of the home used as an office, and the work can be fitted into the daily meal-making and household routine. There are disadvantages, but these are outweighed by the fact that the woman accountant is working at her career at the same time she is working at her traditional role. Accounting permits a woman to keep in touch with the profession while her family matures and prepares her for full-time work when she can accept greater responsibility outside the home.[8]

Miona Hoffman's words, written before the established firms began to hire women, continue to have meaning today. Matching a career and a family has traditionally been one of women's problems. The accounting profession, along with law, is somewhat unique in that the nature of the work permits the building of a local practice at the same time that family commitments are met. Annette Brenner, whose partnership arrangement was described earlier in this chapter, worked for a number of years in this fashion while her sons were going to school. She then went to work part-time for a CPA firm before starting her own practice.

Age Biases

The large national firms also resist hiring women who are older and just entering the profession. Many women who decide to go back to school to study and prepare for the profession after their children are grown find that the larger national firms have no place for them on their career ladders. Age discrimination is illegal, but it exists anyway. Bernice Nathan, for example, graduated and attempted to start a career at the age of 50.[9] She was told by campus recruiters that she was too old, and none of them offered her a job. She sought advice from the Department of Labor, who wrote letters to several of the firms. She was hired by one of them after it received such a letter!

The local practice is today the area in which women have the greatest opportunities. Both the local and the national firms will hire them and give them experience so they can take the certification examination, earn the CPA certificate, and be ready for their own practice. They are then in a position to continue with their present firm, move to another firm, or start their own. If they really want to be their own boss in a profession that permits mixing both family and career opportunities, the local accounting practice is today a viable and attractive option to women.

REFERENCES

1. Brenner, A. and Pizzica, J., "The Partnership Viewpoint," *Pennsylvania CPA Spokesman,* November, 1981, pp. 18–21. This has been reprinted with permission from the PENNSYLVANIA CPA JOURNAL, a publication of the Pennsylvania Institute of Certified Public Accountants.
2. "Women Accountant Groups Hold Joint Annual Meet-

ing," *Journal of Accountancy,* Vol. 146, No. 6, December, 1978, p. 38.

3. "Financial Firms Lead in Naming Women to Boards of Directors," *Burroughs Clearing House,* Vol. 63, No. 8, May, 1979, pp. 4–5.

4. "Women and Minorities Make Big Gains in Status in Banking," *ABA Banking Journal,* October, 1980, p. 20.

5. "Golden State Soon to be Top Financial Center for Women," *Burroughs Clearing House,* Vol. 62, No. 9, June, 1978, p. 8.

6. Brenner and Pizzica, op. cit., p. 20.

7. Henning, J., and Jardin, A., *The Managerial Woman,* New York: Pocket Books, 1977, p. 26.

8. Hoffman, M., "Women Who Should be in Accounting," *The National Public Accountant,* Vol. 18, No. 5, May, 1963, pp. 8–11.

9. Liroff, Jr., "The Delayed Arrival of Bernice Nathan," *The Asset,* Vol. 26, No. 7, July/August, 1978, p. 5.

Professional and Legislative Reactions

Search for Solutions

The AICPA, acting as the official voice of the profession, has recognized that the lack of upward mobility for women within the profession must be faced in a collective way. A committee of the AICPA, entitled the *Future Issues Committee,* was formed for the purpose of identifying and addressing the major problems facing the profession, and the upward mobility of women was one of those selected for study. Professions such as public accounting, law, and medicine usually resist and react slowly to change, and the appointment of a committee was the AICPA's way of beginning the search for solutions to the problem of what to do with so many qualified women in the profession.

The Future Issues Committee spent a considerable amount of time discussing just what the problems were. After identifying fourteen issues, they began to discuss how the profession might begin to take action to solve these problems. In the initial report of this committee, issued late in 1984, they officially recognized the basic problem that is described and illustrated in this book. The committee stated the problem as *How Can the Profession Strengthen the*

158

Upward Mobility of Women in Public Accounting,[1] and made several positive suggestions which could accelerate the acceptance of women. Here is the committee's report on the problem as they saw it and their recommendations:

* Approximately 50 percent of the persons newly hired by public accounting firms are women. Over the long run, more and more women will rise to senior levels in a variety of professions and organizations. Many accountants believe that upward mobility, particularly admission to partnership, is more difficult for women than for men.

Driving Forces

* Women have risen to various levels in accounting firms, but relatively few have been admitted to partnership. Within the past two decades, the number of women entering the profession has increased and, as a consequence, the supply of qualified women now nearly equals the supply of qualified men. The next several years will bring an increasing proportion of women into the potential partner pool. There is a high probability that women will constitute more than half the accounting profession within the next twenty years.
* Admission to partnership is affected by many considerations, notably technical, management, client relationship, and practice development abilities. There is no question about women's technical ability. But traditional beliefs and attitudes regarding other abilities raise questions. For example, are women at a competitive disadvantage in comparison to men in obtaining new audit clients and maintaining existing ones? Is there a women's "network"? Moreover, some partners may believe that men are generally more dedicated to a professional career than are women.
* The employee turnover rate in CPA firms is greater for women than for men, perhaps attributable in part to personal frustration. One reason why professional women find advancement difficult may be society's pressure on women to be the center of family units, including the role of childbearer and child raiser. If a woman is to fulfill both professional and family re-

sponsibilities at the same time, she may need flexibility in her professional work, for example, flexible hours, flexible workdays, or flexible locations.
* The attitudes toward professional women deserve deliberation. Are males as willing and cooperative when their manager is female? What are men's attitudes toward their professional women colleagues?
* Some practitioners think that the issue does not exist, that it has already been solved; that is, women will become partners just as easily as men if their qualifications are similar. On the other hand, others believe that such an attitude is part of the problem, indeed, that it is the central problem.

Options

* The Institute could obtain the opinions and suggestions of men and women in the profession who have had extensive experience in hiring, promoting, and admitting candidates to partnership. Some of those individuals could be constituted as a committee charged with formulating specific plans for assisting firms and the Institute in developing short-range and long-range initiatives in the area.
* The Institute could solicit more information about success stories from firms that have made unusual progress in promoting women to the partnership level. What personnel practices help or hurt?
* Top management of the Institute could use a management-by-objectives approach to bring more women in to work on committees, programs, and similar activities. It could encourage and assist state societies in developing similar programs.
* The Institute could spur wide discussion of the issue by including the subject in programs and in committee activities.
* The Institute could seek cooperation of the American Women's Society of CPA's (AWSCPA) in formulating a program that would enhance the upward mobility of women.
* The Institute could consider developing counseling seminars for professional women of CPA firms to assist them in dealing with the problems they encounter.

There is no question that the organized profession recognizes that a problem exists. Women are being brought into the profession as staff, seniors, and managers in order to maximize the profits of the partner-owners. But what happens when these experienced women have reached a point where they want a piece of the action—when they too want to be partners, to be more in charge of their own destinies? Existing partners are reluctant to split the pie, and if one reads the *Options* portion of the AICPA committee's report, there is very little there that would persuade a male partner to bring a woman into partnership if he accepts any of the stereotyped objections to women enumerated earlier in this book. Talking about the problem will not solve it, additional committees to study the problem will not solve it, and the suggestion of a "management-by-objectives" approach would be ridiculed by anyone who understands how sex discrimination works within the profession. Men partners who do not want a woman as their business partner are not going to admit one into their firm unless they are convinced that it is to their economic advantage to do so, or until some external pressures are brought to bear. External pressures such as the recent sex discrimination legislation enacted by Congress may have an impact greater than the AICPA envisions.

Solutions through Legislation

The numerical growth in the number of women in public accounting coupled with recent sex discrimination legislation has had a gradual but profound impact upon the work attitudes of both men and women in the profession. The Equal Pay Act of 1963, Title VII of the Civil Rights Act of 1964, and several recent Supreme Court decisions concerning women have provided a framework of law within which much of the progress toward equality of the sexes has been accomplished. The earlier violations of these laws occurred at the blue collar level, perhaps because violations were more obvious at that level, and suits were brought for very large sums. When they were won, other companies with similar discriminatory practices quickly began to comply with the regulations.

The Equal Pay Act of 1963 was an amendment to the Fair Labor Standards Act, one of the early labor laws which dates back into the 1940's. It prohibits discrimination on the basis of sex in the payment of wages for work requiring equal skills, effort, and responsibility, and performed under similar working conditions. The disclosure of the woman's name need not be made in a suit brought under this act, a provision placed there for her protection while the suit is being tried.

Title VII of the Civil Rights Act of 1964 is extremely broad in scope and prohibits discrimination in all phases of employment, including age, race, sex, and national origin. A suit was settled under this provision for $38 million against AT&T, principally for discrimination against women.

Most of the pay and hiring discrimination suits were brought at the blue collar level because discrimination was more difficult to prove at the white collar level. At the white collar level, each person's work assignments tend to be somewhat different, and each job requires slightly different skills and training. Public accounting, however, has similar levels of responsibility within the beginning staff, senior, or managerial levels, and pay differentials were not uncommon at the time these laws came into effect. Many of the women we interviewed told of pay differences that were straightened out when legislation existed to back up the individual's complaint.

These discrepancies were usually taken care of privately; lawsuits were uncommon within the public accounting profession. Those that were brought were quickly settled out of court, for the firm did not want to risk a loss of client confidence. The conservative nature of public accounting is such that a lawsuit of any kind against a firm is considered a disaster.

While it may be a sad commentary on our society, forceful legislation has thus far been the only effective technique for initiating change in the traditional role of women in a work environment. Public accounting is no exception; legislation has had its impact upon hiring and pay practices in that profession. A nation cannot effectively legislate morals, but in the area of discrimination it can bring into existence laws that spell out the nature of equality and that provide the basis for insuring that equality is maintained. Assuming that these definitions are correct and the enforcement methods realistic, having the legislation in place will, over time, shift public morals in the desired direction.

Rosalyn Yalow, the Nobel Prize winner in medicine, had this to say about women's right to equal opportunities and the role of legislation:

> I think we must accept the proposition that the problems associated with what I have termed social discrimination may never disappear completely and, at best, are likely to change quite slowly. They are not easily solved, and what is on our lips may not be in our psyches. We have a right to expect, however, that the laws of the land will protect our rights for equal opportunity. This does not mean setting aside places for women who are not fully competitive for the roles to which they aspire. Redress for past wrongs should not provide bonuses for the undeserving.[2]

There is reason to believe that the legislation placed into effect in the early 1970's has had a bearing on the opening up of the accounting profession to women. This is especially true of the Title VII amendment to the Civil Rights Act, which prohibited discrimination in the hiring of women. Both large and small public accounting firms were hiring only men prior to that time. This Act, passed in 1972, coincided almost exactly with the willingness of the large firms to recruit women on university campuses and offer a limited number of positions to them. When these few worked out exceedingly well, the firms increased the number of offers they made to women, so that, some five or six years later (by the late 1970's), they were hiring women in sizeable numbers. What exact impact the 1972 legislation had on hiring practices within the profession can only be surmised, for there were other forces at work also. The timing coincidence, however, is too strong to have happened by pure chance.

It is also of interest that smaller public accounting firms did not begin to hire women until the larger firms had broken the ice. Smaller firms with less than twenty-five employees were not subject to the Title VII amendment during its early period, and thus strong legal pressures were not exerted on them to follow a stringent employment policy. There are more small CPA firms under twenty-five employees than there are large firms, and the fact that small firms waited several years before beginning to accept women is further evidence of the impact of the 1972 legislation upon the hiring practices of the profession.

Prior to the 1970's many of the CPA firms who recruited on campus would not even interview women. Title VII prohibits a firm from restricting its recruiting to a single sex, race, or color. It was about this time the firms began to interview qualified women as well as men. As has been indicated in earlier chapters, they did not hire many at first—many practice offices restricted their work forces to the "token woman." Further, Title VII prohibits a firm from exclusion of one sex, even though customers may prefer the other sex. This provision has undoubtedly had a dampening effect upon the age-old argument that clients will not accept women auditors. When, in the latter half of the 1970's, clients did not really object to those first token women auditors, the number of women hired was increased substantially.

Perhaps the lack of client resistance to women auditors was also a function of the Title VII requirements. There is also the possibility that the controllers and treasurers of client companies who select the company's auditors, almost all of whom are male, saw the handwriting on the wall concerning equality of the sexes and accepted women when they might not have a few years earlier. No one knows for sure, but these are the circumstances which lead us to the conclusion that legislation such as Title VII did play a very strong role in the opening up of the profession to women.

The provisions of Title VII continue to be strengthened and refined by the courts. Many of the earlier cases have made their way through the court system, some never going beyond a District Court, but many reaching the Supreme Court. One such case that will impact the public accounting profession was decided by the Supreme Court in May 1984. It concerned sex discrimination in the selection of partners.

Legislation on Selection of Partners

Professions such as law and public accounting utilize the partnership form of organization. They have long held that selection of one's partners is an individual matter not subject to governmental interference or regulation. That right was believed to be protected by the First and the Fourteenth Amendments of the Constitution, which provide for freedom of association and expression. These constitutional safeguards have been offered as sufficient grounds to justify an individual's right to select, without constraint, another individual as his or her partner, and conversely to refuse partnership to another. The Supreme Court held in the case of *Hishon v. King and Spalding*[3] that Title VII does cover such decisions, and that sex discrimination in the selection of partners is no longer valid.

Moving from the manager level to partnership in the firm is the one step in the career ladder that has been the most difficult for women in public accounting. The existing men partners have been willing to have women work for them, but not to be their business partners. Women have been accepted within the profession at the staff and supervisory levels for almost a decade, and there has been little resistance to women auditors by either clients or the partners who own the CPA firm. There has been, however, tremendous resistance to "admitting them into the firm" as partners, even though they have the experience and talents. This last major barrier now appears to have been broken by the *Hishon* case, although insufficient time has passed since the Court's decision to determine the full impact.

In the *Hishon* case, Elizabeth Hishon, an attorney just graduated from law school, was hired by the law firm of King and Spalding. She was told, as part of the recruiting discussion, that new associates who received satisfactory evaluations were promoted to partnership on a fair and equal basis. The law firm was a large one, with some fifty associates working for it in addition to Ms. Hishon. She received satisfactory evaluations, but after she had been with the firm the usual number of years and had sufficient experience, she was denied a partnership, even though men with equal qualifications were being made partners.

When Elizabeth filed suit, claiming sex discrimination, the District Court dismissed the case, ruling that partners have the right to select their own partners and that Title VII did not apply. The Supreme Court found differently and reversed the District Court, holding that indeed the sex discrimination provisions of Title VII do apply to the selection of partners when admittance to partnership is implied in the employment agreement. The defense of the existing partners was that their right of association is protected by the First Amendment of the Constitution, and that no person should be forced to associate with another against his or her will. Justice Powell, in the Court's decision, stated that an obligation was assumed at the time of employment, that it was voluntarily assumed by the partners at that time, and that enforcement of this obligation without regard to sex does not impair the defendant's right of association. In essence, the Court was saying that elevation to partnership cannot be denied because of sex when an employee is brought into the firm with partnership held out as the natural consequence of satisfactory performance.

Public accounting firms utilize an eventual partnership as one of the selling points in recruiting young university graduates. The admittance of women to partnership is stoutly resisted, but the *Hishon* case should remove the consideration of sex from that decision. If the woman's progress with the firm is satisfactory, she should now have an opportunity for advancement to partner equal to that of men managers. Elevation to the level of manager is itself very strong evidence of satisfactory progress, for there are usually at least six or seven years of experience and two or three promotion points that must be passed before one becomes a manager. Unless the proportion of women and men who are admitted to partnership equals the proportion of women and men managers who are eligible, there are rather obvious grounds for claims of sex discrimination.

Affirmative Action

The decision of the Supreme Court in this case calls for affirmative action on the part of existing partners to provide women with the kind of experience that will place them in equal contention for partnership positions. This means assigning them clients and problem areas that will provide professional growth and stimulation. It also means educating clients to accept women auditors, in those isolated cases where such education is needed, that professional competency is not sex-dependent. If the ruling is to be applied as the Court intended, perhaps a partner should refuse to remove a woman from the audit, even though the client expresses an objection to women auditors. Such objection would rarely happen today, however, for clients are usually well aware of the sex discrimination provisions of the law.

Business Organizations

Another Supreme Court decision was handed down on July 3, 1984, which has direct implications for the career development of women in public accounting. In this case, the Court held that all-male organizations such as the U.S. Jaycees must admit women. The decision was unanimous, and the Court held that organizations which are primarily operated as commercial or business organizations must admit women. Those that are of a purely social nature were not included in the definition of a business or commercial organization. However, one of the primary tests of whether the organization is business or social is the handling of membership fees. If employers pay the dues of the members, or, if a large percentage of members deduct the dues on their tax returns as a business expense, the organization is considered a business one. This definition thus includes most country clubs, luncheon clubs, and civic organizations, such as the Rotary Club, Jaycees, and Lions Club.

The argument given by employers in paying the dues of such organizations is that membership is valuable and provides a source of contacting new clients and customers. Women have been at a distinct disadvantage when membership in such organizations has not been available to them, since they could not develop new business for their firm as effectively as men could. This has been one of the arguments given for not admitting women into partnership positions—that they cannot bring in new business, as a partner must. Opening up the membership of these organizations to women thus removes another barrier.

Similar to the *Hishon* case, the Supreme Court reversed a ruling of a District Court which held that these organizations had a right to decide who would be members. The defense offered by the Jaycees in this case was the same as that used in *Hishon*—that of the right of association. The Supreme Court held that the business nature of these organizations made them subject to Title VII, and that there could be no sex discrimination.

Justice Sandra Day O'Connor, the first woman to sit on the Supreme Court, qualified her opinion. She said in her qualification that certain clubs should be afforded more latitude in picking their members, such as those providing training of outdoor survival skills or participation in community service, when the activity is intended to develop good morals, reverence for a higher diety, patriotism, and a desire for self-improvement. The authors fail to understand this distinction and believe, as did the other members of the

Court, that if the organization is business-oriented, it should be free of sex discrimination.

Now that the Title VII provisions have had a dozen or more years to be enforced and interpreted by the courts, the trend has been toward elimination of the more subtle forms of discrimination, such as those covered in the two Supreme Court cases discussed here. The obvious types of discrimination were ferreted out in the early years of administering the statute, and today the more hidden, insidious types of discrimination are being removed. As we indicated at the beginning of this chapter, the laws of the land lay the foundation for slow but inescapable shifts in the morals and prejudices of society. The acceptance of women in public accounting is not yet fully realized, but giant steps have been taken. Barriers are crumbling day by day, and there is gathering evidence that the progress the public accounting profession will realize during this decade will exceed that of the one just past in removing the types of discrimination that face professional women.

REFERENCES

1. American Institute of Certified Public Accountants, "Upward Mobility of Women," *Major Issues for the CPA Profession and the AICPA: A Report by the AICPA Future Issues Committee,* New York, 1984, pp. 17–19. Copyright © 1984 by the American Institute of Certified Public Accountants, Inc. Reprinted with permission.
2. Yalow, R. "A Winner (Nobel Prize) Talks About the Status of Her Sex," *Across the Board: The Conference Board Magazine,* Vol. 16, No. 9, September, 1979, pp. 54–59.
3. *Hishon v. King and Spalding,* May 22, 1984. See also Seiler, R., and Horvitz, J., "The Partnership Decision— The Hishon Case," *The CPA Journal,* Vol. 55, No. 1, January, 1985, pp. 12–19.

Discrimination and Sex Stereotyping in Public Accounting

The assertion that women are different from men hardly needs to be justified here. Biological differences are the most obvious, but the most critical differences to the career development of women are not physical—they are produced by societal sex-role stereotyping. Both women and men are social creatures, and the roles they assume within society are in large part determined by what we are taught that our roles should be. The teaching of what women's roles are and what men's roles are begins in the cradle and is reinforced throughout life in both direct and subtle ways. Changing an adult's concept of sex roles is difficult and can be accomplished only over a long period of time. Unfortunately, in conservative professions such as public accounting, these changes come gradually and somewhat painfully.

Internal and External Impediments

Today women begin their careers in public accounting on more or less equal terms with men—but their progress from that point on is impeded by ingrained and often subconscious attitudes concerning the proper role of the two sexes. Social scientists who study sex-role stereotyping separate the impediments that affect the career development of women into two classes: the individual attitudes within the woman herself, and the attitudes of society.

Internal impediments are the result of women's own sex-role concepts. This individual component includes not only personal attitudes and values, but also interests, abilities, and knowledge of opportunity. The social factor includes political, economical, and social attributes which delimit the range of expression of the individual. Women find these external impediments at many points in their work environments. In public accounting, the strongest impediment is the biased view about women still held by those males in leadership positions within the profession.

One of the more significant social factors is the fact that society continues to influence both men and women from childhood to fit certain molds and to play certain roles. Although there are forces at work in our society that lessen the extent of this subtle programming, it is still relatively strong.

Several sex-role concepts that have been internalized by women and supported by men have had a stronger impact upon the profession of public accounting than upon some of the other professions, and we have chosen to concentrate on those. Several of the more significant concepts are listed below. Anyone familiar with sex-role stereotyping can tell at a glance that they are more myth than truth. However, a significant portion of our society continues to believe that they are true.

* Men, more than women, have natural business leadership ability.
* Women were meant to be mothers and wives, and business leadership positions are not their natural place in life.
* Women have less pressure to work, for they have the option to select wifehood rather than a business career.
* Women have a fear of success.

The continued acceptance by both women and men of the "appropriate roles of the sexes" is the greatest deterrent to women's acceptance in the professions. There are many who do not realize or who have not internalized into their value structures the basic truth that most human beings seek a creative, fulfilling life, and further, that the traditional roles of mother and wife do not necessarily provide these ingredients. Regardless of what one does, or what type of work one undertakes, it must contribute to the individual's identity and self-esteem and must bring order and meaning to the individual's life.

Subtle Role Formation

In our affluent society, we are just beginning to learn that having an interesting and fulfilling job is more important than having a job that pays well. There is also evidence that our society is beginning to recognize that continued growth in stature and responsibility is also an essential ingredient for one's well being and individual fulfillment.

But our childhood programming gets in the way! Study after study has shown that most women, as well as men, would prefer a man as "boss," other things being equal. There is a kind of subconscious respect given to the male figurehead, and many of us are programmed from childhood to accept males as the "natural" leaders. Everything from the movies we watch to the textbooks we use in the first grade points to male dominance in leadership positions. In a business environment, this creates competition among men for leadership roles. Women, who also want that leadership spot, tend to be inhibited from fully entering into similar competition. A female executive in the garment industry, one of the toughest industries in our economy, addressed this point when she said, "When women lose their starstruck, awe-struck attitude that men who have made it in the business are necessarily smarter than they are, they'll be that much nearer successful careers themselves."[1]

Successful women in the business world learn and internalize early the fact that men have no natural business ability that they themselves do not have. Earlier in this book a number of studies were described showing that women have not only equal but greater abilities to perform the technical and administrative work required in the public accounting profession. Women learn during their college experience that they can match men in the technical aspects of the profession. Their classroom performance assures them of at least equality in that arena. But upon leaving college and entering the public accounting profession, women find themselves in an environment where they are competing in more than just technical areas. In this new competition, their self-confidence and belief in themselves as equals in non-professional areas become critical. At this point the subtle programming mentioned earlier begins to take its toll; if a woman feels that men have some kind of natural edge in managerial activities, she will start her career handicapped.

Traditional Sex-Role Concepts

A century ago women were encouraged from early childhood that their primary responsibility as a young adult was to produce the next generation, through childbearing and family activities. Men were encouraged to feel that their primary responsibility was to provide the physical necessities of food, clothing, and shelter that are needed to maintain the current and coming generation. Today, however, since our society is approaching zero population growth, the physical necessities and comforts of life assume a greater share of our efforts. Thus our society, as well as that of other industrialized countries, is in a position to break free of the traditional attitudes about the roles of the wife and mother.

The traditional attitudes, important in less complex societies, required that men and women function primarily as a couple. Today, in our much more complex society, the freedom to function as an individual is becoming more important. We still, however, retain a certain sense of propriety (even if questionable), handed down from prior generations, that men should not do "women's work," and women should not compete in the "man's world." These traditional attitudes still make many men reluctant to be gentle, and many women reluctant to be aggressive. Thus the ghosts of the past have not been completely obliterated in most of us.

Hulene Foster, partner of Touche Ross & Co., gave her view of how she combined her technical skills with a positive attitude to deal with biases in order to succeed within her profession:

> I believe much of success in the final analysis must be attributed to the attitude of the aspiring person. If I had believed that I was not going to be treated fairly by my superiors, then I would have been looking for evidence to support that belief. Instead, I believed that if my performance warranted promotions and raises then I would receive such. However, I did always feel that my performance had to be better than my male peers, but I guess I never blamed the male dominated profession for my having to be better. You see, they were conditioned on stereotypes of women. My obligation to myself was to show them I was not the stereotype, and I did!

Impact on Formal Education

The subtle influencing of women to feel that public accounting is a man's profession begins in public schools and continues through college. Women teachers abound in elementary and secondary education, but university accounting courses are predominately taught by men. Studies have shown that 88 percent of accounting professors are men.[2] Almost all of the examples and class problems worked out in accounting courses and included in accounting texts use men's names for CPA partners and for the firm's clients. Rare indeed is it that a woman's name appears in these textbooks. The popular cost accounting textbook by Horngren, undoubtedly the most widely used text in its area for over twenty-five years, rarely mentioned women in its examples through the first three editions. Only in the latest editions has he begun to utilize women in administrative positions in some of his examples.

Other leading texts continue to use men exclusively in their discussions. The underrepresentation of women in textbooks at the university level, and especially women in administrative positions, has been documented in several studies.[3] The combination of predominately male accounting instructors and an almost universal use of male examples in accounting texts continues subtly to reinforce the supposition begun in elementary school that public accounting is a man's domain.

Many universities are beginning to recognize their responsibility to women. This is evidenced by their hiring more women professors and providing coverage of the problems which women encounter when they enter the business community. There is also an effort in many colleges to provide better career counseling for women. Many university counselors are women with business experience who can provide advice on subjects such as how a woman can assert herself without losing points, how to fight salary discrimination successfully, the appropriate dress codes, and "office politics."

Formal Study of Women's Problem Areas

Universities are partly to blame for the fact that women leave their accounting programs retaining a bit of this subconscious fear of entering the "man's world of public accounting." A recent survey of universities offering degrees in business (all of these include courses in accounting), revealed that only one-fourth of the universities responding had an organized course of study that dealt with the problems women encounter when they enter the business world.[4] This study indicated that another one-fourth recognized the existence of the problem and were thinking of including it somewhere in their curriculum. Therefore, only one-half of the surveyed universities recognize in a formal manner the need for a course of study dealing with the unique problems women face as they enter the business world. One of the more frequently stated justifications of those that did not have such a course was, "Such a course is not needed because men and women need the same training to compete equally in the business world." This is a some what ostrich-like approach to structuring university curricula!

The "Women in Management" Course

The title of the course, when this topic is covered by a separate course, is usually "Women in Management," and interestingly, some 26 percent of the existing courses are taught by male instructors! The topics covered normally include the following:
* Strategies for bringing women into management
* Analysis of sex differences
* Institutional barriers for women
* Women in leadership
* Human relations in action
* Successful role models in administration
* Developing supervisory and managerial skills
* Role conflict
* The socialization process: its managerial implications
* "Corporate lib"
* State and federal laws
* Issues of equality
* A woman in a man's world

The relatively low percentage of schools offering coverage of this important topic indicates that deans and/or faculties lack a perceived need for this subject matter. However, since the success of women at the professional and management levels depends upon their ability to adjust and cope with an environment that has largely been designed and defined by men, one would think that the need is obvious. That university deans and faculties do not recognize the need is more surprising than the existence of bias among established male public accounting practitioners.

The fact that men students are frequently found in this course is one of the silver linings of the cloud created by insufficient university coverage of this topic. Awareness on the part of men is an important step in altering their ingrained sex-role concepts. In addition, some of the courses are taught by a team of two professors, one man and one woman. This arrangement permits a great deal of interplay where the viewpoint of one is either challenged or expanded upon by the other and provides an excellent learning experience.

Continuing Education Role

For those women and men who have already completed their formal education and begun their professional careers, there is a need for some type of experience similar to the "Women in Management" course offered at the university level. Since public accountants in almost all of the fifty states are subject to continuing education requirements, a seminar on the same topics covered in the university course could be arranged, utilizing a conference approach and structured to suit practitioners. One manager advocated such a course in the systems development area,[5] and even listed the topics that should be covered. The program was given the suggested title of "The Let's-Get-It-Equal Program," where each gender learns about the attitudes and expectations of the other. Such a program could include the following topics:

* Exposure of some of the attitudes that put women at a disadvantage—for example, that they do not develop sufficient career commitments
* How leadership tasks could be structured to eliminate irrelevant sex-role typing
* Establishing objective performance goals
* Developing team building skills
* Assistance in career planning
* Training individuals to solve conflicts through information methods, to manage conflict constructively without negative feelings

* How to understand and improve the structure and climate in a public accounting firm
* Role models; how to learn from one, how to be one

The impact that could be realized by requiring every male and female member of the public accounting profession to sit through such a full one- or two-day program, taught by experienced conference leaders, can only be imagined! For that matter, members of any profession could benefit from such exposure. The legal profession, for example, has a set of problems not too dissimilar to those found today in public accounting.

Jane Kay, an experienced and successful organizer of such conferences, described her views, which were a distillation of experiences gleaned from the 3,000 women who have attended her sessions. She said:

> Many found that, as women, they need to be much better qualified and work much harder to equal the progress made by men. I am constantly amazed at the number of women who readily accept this criterion and are willing to meet it. Those who give up or rebel are definitely in the minority. As a matter of fact, some women seem willing to stand aside for their male peers, even when the women are well aware that they, themselves, are as well or better qualified. Ironically, the progress women make may depend on the attitudes of less-qualified men in management toward promoting better qualified women.[6]

Socialization of Women

Another of the attitudes listed at the beginning of this chapter was that women have more options available to them than men, primarily through the possibility of marriage and letting the husband be the source of financial support. Having such an option, according to some researchers, affects the timing of the career decisions of women. That women make career choices later in life than men has been documented in several studies reported earlier in this book, but whether this timing difference is due to having more choices available to them has not been confirmed. Anne Lewis, writing in the *Journal of College Placement,* argued that the decision comes later as a result of the early childhood programming that women receive. She said:

> That was my problem—women college graduates were over-educated and under-socialized. They were educated alongside all of the men who had now gone on to law school, or med school, or management training programs. Their socialization had not included the thought of professional school. Although they were willingly sent to the same undergraduate schools with their brothers, their parents did not really intend that they should do the same things with that education. The colleges they went to trained them the same as the men, but then forgot to make any adjustments for the realities of the working world. In effect, women learned as men, but upon graduation they were expected to do either menial tasks or be satisfied as wives and mothers.[7]

Anne went on to define the term under-socialization as being the difference between job orientation and career orientation. "A job," she said, "is employment that one takes in order to make money, but a career is infused with elements of motivation, aspiration, and self-satisfaction." When one takes a job, one feels that he or she is filling a role in a business. When one works at a career, one feels that he or she is making a contribution, and, at the same time, working to improve professionally and intellectually.

Women are socialized to "take a job," rather than "enter a profession," and sex-role stereotyping is the impetus behind that conditioning. Even though a woman may be educated in the same university program as a man, she may be under-socialized for the position she takes when she graduates. She does not accept a job which is not up to her level of education, but she is conditioned to taking a job, not embarking on a career. After she has worked for a while, perhaps years, she realizes that the work satisfaction which she innately needs comes from the commitment, aspiration, and motivation that accrue through a career, not just a job. Thus studies on the timing of career decisions have revealed that for many women, the decision comes later. A more accurate reflection, however, would be that the studies report the result of a socialization process that takes place later in a woman's life.

Fear of Success

Fear of success is another of the attitudes which were listed at the beginning of this chapter as being an impediment to women in public accounting. This psychological attribute was found in the research of Matina Horner, who went on to become president of Radcliffe College.[8] She found a widespread "fear of success" among talented women and demonstrated that, whereas both men and women have a fear of failure, many women exhibit a similar fear of success.

She conceptualized it as a latent, stable personality characteristic that is established early in one's personality development, during acquisition of the female's sex-role identity. The motive to avoid success in the business world, "consists in a predisposition to become anxious in achievement-oriented situations that are inherently competitive and therefore are not 'feminine.'" If women were more aggressive toward obtaining a greater piece of the pie, she argues, the movement of women into public accounting to the current point where they constitute 25 percent of the professionals in the field would have been a lot "noisier" than it was. There is little doubt that early childhood programming has resulted in this fear of being successful in what the fearful individual must consider a man's world. The existence of this subconscious attitude is perhaps one of the greatest tragedies of our times!

Discrimination in Professions

The temporary acceptance of women during World War II presents some interesting questions concerning discrimination in professional settings. Several theories may be advanced to explain why discrimination exists in a profession. One of these focuses on the competition for scarce resources, including wealth and power. Limiting a profession to a few insures a monopoly for those few. Selective recruitment, from the same ethnic group or from the same sex, keeps the privileges and other benefits that have been accumulated within that existing group.

Another theory centers on the nature of groups themselves and the ways in which they form and maintain their identity. Professions are communities of individuals, and their professional expertise separates them from other groups and provides cohesion. Professions are careful to be sure others do not overstep into their boundaries, and each profession publicizes its outer edges. Confrontations with outsiders, and even with their own deviant members, result from these boundary placements. The "we" and "they" syndrome builds as a result. The male and female separation in a profession is an example of this kind of human tendency.

Justification for discrimination sometimes comes merely through the act of defining certain people as insiders and others as outsiders. Rationalizations frequently follow the exclusion, rather than account for it. When the existing rationalization changes and becomes dated, an absurd new one will arise to ensure that the division remains. In accounting, when the rationalization that clients would not tolerate female auditors was disproved, in its place came the rationalization that women are not career-oriented and not willing to pay the price to build a career—that marriage and children could not be compatible with professional careers.

When people accept one of these rationalizations, they perpetuate the hidden injuries of class, which make one numb and destroy the energy to plunge ahead. At the very least, the spirit is dampened and the will to forge ahead is reduced. Discrimination causes hidden injuries, and because these injuries are not physically apparent, even the persons suffering may deny that they exist. Many of the women we interviewed denied a salary bias when salary data were not generally available to them. They had denied to themselves the possibility of a bias. Some of the women we interviewed described waking up to the possibility of bias in both salary and assignments only after they had left a firm to take another position.

Discrimination can induce trauma in a way similar to the consequences of chronic disaster. A chronic disaster is one that gathers force slowly and insidiously, creeping around one's defenses rather than smashing through them. One is unable to mobilize normal defenses against the threat, sometimes because he or she has elected consciously or unconsciously to ignore it, and sometimes because he or she cannot do anything to avoid it, in any case.

Feminine or Masculine?

Women who are successful in public accounting, like successful women in other male-dominated professions, are sometimes perceived as being of the tough, aggressive type, the kind who hide their femininity behind a cloak. Such a misconception is prevalent in many areas of business management. Those who believe this myth are indeed under a delusion.

The incorrect perception of women accountants as being nonfeminine, or conversely, as being of the retiring, shrinking-violet type, has plagued the profession for decades. Consider, for example, this piece taken from the *New York Sun* issue of August 23, 1937:

> Julia Benton Hopkins, who, armed only with a school diploma and degrees in accountancy, became the first and only woman examiner ever appointed by the powerful board of governors of the Federal Reserve System in Washington. Some 200 veteran banking and financial experts comprise its staff of examiners. Women for some reason have been slow to approach so technical a field.
>
> This charming lady is the very antithesis of the popular conception of such an expert! Modishly gowned, with a tip-tilted hat at just the right angle, she urges all

women to be equally true to type. "There is nothing to be gained by imitating men," says a deliberate voice that hints of the South. "The consideration and tact of the drawing room is just as valuable in business."

Mrs. Hopkins' meteoric success is not based on feminine qualities alone. It is founded on a thorough preparation in public accounting, steady judgment, ability to understand figures and attention to details.

The dramatic hour of the 1933 banking crisis found her beginning work with the Federal Reserve Board, where experience has increased her conviction that abundant opportunities lie in wait for women, as well as men accountants.

"Go after the big salaries," is the summary of Julia Hopkins' advice and, "if the attentive beginner follow it to the full, she will keep her toes in things feminine."[9]

In general, women professionals today neither flaunt nor hide femininity—they are simply professionals performing the task for which they were trained. They develop an ability to adapt, have a strong commitment to their work, and are intelligent and willing to work. Accounting, like other professions, requires a sharp mind and an alertness in excess of that required in nonprofessional positions. The women we encountered while completing this study were like any other group of well-educated and well-read women. Their constant contact with the public also made them aware of personal appearance, and this awareness was evident in both dress and manner.

REFERENCES

1. *Women's Wear Daily,* October 21, 1975.
2. Reha, R., "Preparing Women for Management Roles," *Business Horizons,* Vol. 22, No. 2, April, 1979, pp. 68–71.
3. Astin, H., Susiewick, N., and Dweck, S., *Women: A Bibliography on Their Education and Careers,* Washington, D.C.: Human Service Press, 1971, pp. 12–15.
4. Reha, op. cit.
5. Koehn, H., "Attitude: The Success Element for Women

in Business," *Journal of Systems Management,* Vol. 27, No. 3, March, 1976.

6. Kay, J., "What Do These Women Want?" *University of Michigan Business Review,* Vol. 27, No. 3, May, 1975, pp. 9–12.

7. Lewis, A., "Things That College Never Taught Me," *Journal of College Placement,* Vol. 35, No. 2, Winter, 1975, pp. 52–55.

8. *Time,* March 19, 1979.

9. *New York Sun,* August 23, 1937.

Contemporary Problems

The solution to a problem often brings with it new and different problems. This is especially evident in the acceptance of women into the accounting profession, for a host of new problems and issues have arisen. These issues range from personal problems, such as meshing the rearing of children with the demands of the profession, to those more general in nature, such as the social interaction of men and women working and traveling together. This chapter addresses these issues, including both those that impact on the profession directly and those that are more personal in nature.

Stereotyping at Work

The effects of sex-role stereotyping are subtle and pervasive, as discussed in the previous chapter. But there are also effects of stereotyping that show up in everyday events, which can sometimes be embarrassing as well as frustrating for both men and women. Susan Butler, a partner in the New York office of Arthur Andersen & Co., has presented a number of such incidents in a speech which she gives to different professional groups. Her message clearly illustrates that in sex-role stereotyping women are as apt to jump to the wrong conclusion as men. She relates the time she called another partner in her firm and a different male voice answered. It was not the person to whom she wanted to talk, and she immediately assumed that she was talking to one of the seniors or managers who worked for that partner and happened to be in his office at that moment. As it turned out, it was his new male secretary! She had made a mistake similar in nature to the one made by an airline reservation clerk whom Susan Butler had called to make her travel arrangements. The airline clerk said, "And when does HE want to return?"

Another new situation is created by the woman who picks up the check at a restaurant. For many men this is no problem because they realize the bill will be paid by the woman's firm through her expense account. Others, though, perhaps because their male egos will not let them accept women as truly equal professionals, are extremely uncomfortable in such situations. Of course, the woman has as much obligation to pick up the bill as a man does in a similar situation. When a man cannot gracefully allow the woman to pay the bill, everyone senses the awkwardness of the situation. Even when she is permitted to take the check, a large proportion of men feel that it is necessary to make such comments as "Well, I guess it's all right for a woman to pay the check," or "Okay, but it doesn't seem right for you to take the check."

Telephone calls are another possible source of problems for the woman professional. A telephone call after work or on weekends to a client or an associate's home is often necessary to clear up a point or confirm an event or appointment. For men, calling a male associate whose wife answers the telephone is no big deal, but when a woman is calling a male associate, suspicion could result. "Who is this woman calling my husband during the weekend?" the wife may wonder. As Susan Butler relates in her speech, it is appropriate for the woman making the weekend call to learn the name of the associate's wife, so that when the call is made she can say, "Hello, Mary, this is Susan from Arthur Andersen, and I need to confirm an appointment for Monday.

Is Bob there?" At least the wife knows who is calling, and why.

Problems in Professional Organizations

The effects of stereotyping men as natural business leaders are evident in the professional public accounting societies, such as state societies and their local chapters. Underrepresentation of women in positions of leadership is chronic in such organizations. Shirley Dahl, a partner in the Los Angeles office of Price Waterhouse and a former president of AWSCPA, is quoted as saying[1] in a very perceptive report on the status of women in the profession, "I fought an uphill battle with state societies that were not willing to allow women in leadership roles. Those roles enable women to learn the very valuable skills of public speaking, leading and directing." Half the women interviewed in this report stated that state and national public accounting professional groups did not allow them to participate fully in activities that develop skills needed in manager, partner, and director positions. The general consensus of these women was that positions of leadership in the associations are reserved for the old-time CPA's who will never change their attitudes toward women.

The generation of public accountants who are currently entering the profession will undoubtedly change this condition, since the men have more contemporary attitudes. In addition, the increasing proportion of women in the organizations will have an impact. Shirley Dahl predicted that in about ten years a significant change might begin to take place. Many think it may take a bit longer, but it certainly must happen eventually.

The Open Door Policy

Women are not only more anxious to serve, but they make themselves more available to serve on professional society committees and boards. Their availability is consistent with their work styles. A recent study of the availability of men and women executives to those who work with them concluded that female managers were twice as accessible as male managers. The study that provided this conclusion used as a measure of accessibility the individual's open or closed door policy, numbers and types of interruptions, reactions to interruptions, absences from the office, use of secretaries to screen out potential interruptions, and encouragement of their subordinates to telephone or contact them at home or after work with business problems. The study found that men almost consciously maintained a barrier, while the women consciously removed the barriers to accessibility.

Women	Men
I try to answer the phone rather than have my secretary say, "She is not available."	My secretary's main responsibility is to limit my availability.
All the girls have my phone number and can call me at any time. I cannot say no.	She screens out requests for appointments.
I can never be too available. Denying requests for my time would be seen as neglect.	It depends who wants to reach me. If my boss is calling, I'm very accessible.
I care about my employees and I go out of my way to assure myself that there is no trouble.	I'm not available enough my employees say. I always look busy and they don't wish to disturb me.
My door is always open. They can walk in any time. I don't mind their interruptions—it's part of my job.	I believe in keeping my distance.
	Certain members of my staff come to me with details they could handle themselves that don't require any action on my part.

The following representative statements were made by the 68 male and 102 female managers included in the study.[2] This study concluded that a male manager who obviously cares about his employees and pays attention to their needs through an "open door" policy may risk being viewed as soft by his peers or his male superiors. Concern with worker satisfaction could be construed as concern for the feelings of employees, and men, through the conditioning and programming of early childhood, tend to be uncomfortable with this emotion at work. Women on the other hand, follow their earlier socialization and tend to give more freely and to be more concerned about others. Thus they follow a more "open door" policy of leadership.

There are both advantages and disadvantages to the open door policy. One of the disadvantages is that it places emphasis upon present problems and takes time away from the planning aspects of the job. This is of some interest in public accounting, where planning, scheduling, simultaneous management of several complex jobs is the primary activity of seniors, managers, and partners. One of the more difficult steps up the ladder for women in public accounting is from staff, where they utilize the technical materials learned in their formal university training, to managerial positions beginning at the senior level. This transition requires that considerable attention be given to the planning aspects of the job. The traditional values instilled during childhood makes this transition more difficult for women, as evidenced by their more natural inclinations toward open door policies of leadership.

Dress Codes

Accounting, being the conservative and careful profession that it is, necessarily promotes conservative dress. Women in public accounting have come about as close as any single group to adopting what John Malloy calls in his book *The Woman's Dress for Success Book* the "woman's business uniform." He stated that the uniform should be a skirted suit and blouse, and in most cases the suit should be dark, with a contrasting blouse. There are few exceptions to this style of dress among Big Eight women partners.

John Malloy, continuing his argument for the woman's uniform, states that the world of finance, and that certainly includes accounting, has led in the move toward a more uniform dress code. He writes.

> This outfit will give business women a look of authority, which is precisely what they need. If women are to enjoy widespread success in all industries, they must adopt this uniform. It is their best hope.
>
> One indication that the skirted suit will be widely adopted is the fact that in many industries it already has been. In banking and finance, particularly on Wall Street, few successful women would consider regularly wearing anything but the skirted suit.
>
> When this uniform is accepted by large numbers of businesswomen, as I am confident it will be, it will be attacked ferociously by the enemies of women, many of whom are themselves women. The uniform issue will become an acid test to see which women are going to support other women in their executive ambitions.

Malloy's opinions must certainly be supported by accounting firms, as evidenced by the fact that his article appeared in Peat, Marwick, Mitchell's house organ *World*. He writes very specifically for the accounting profession in that article, as follows:

THE ACCOUNTANT'S UNIFORM

> The best uniform for women accountants is a solid medium gray suit with a white blouse. Second best is a charcoal gray suit with a white blouse, and third is a light gray suit with a white blouse. Quite obviously, the colors an accountant should be flying are gray and white.
>
> Solid blue tests well too. Navy and medium-range blue suits with white blouses are the best of the blues.
>
> Tweed does not test well on women accountants.
>
> Women accountants should not carry handbags. They should carry a large, leather, masculine attache case with a dial lock. The case should be at least four inches deep.
>
> We found that when women accountants arrived in

client offices dressed in conservative, skirted suits, carrying the right attache cases, and got right down to business with little chit-chat, they got a very high rating.

GLASSES SPELL AUTHORITY

After reading a research report on glasses, a woman in a corporation I consult for looked up at me and said, "Damn it. I've got twenty-twenty vision."

She had just discovered that our research indicates that glasses—the right glasses—add weight to a woman's face and consequently make her look considerably more authoritative.

I have seen small, ineffective women gain effectiveness simply by wearing windowpanes with proper frames. I've never recommended that to a client, but I know it works.

The right glasses have plastic or bone frames of moderate size. The frames should match the woman's hair if she is a brunette. If she is a blonde or a redhead, her glasses should not pick up the tint of her hair. Her frames should be a dark, unaesthetic brown. Avoid wire rims.

For the same reason that glasses work very well for the business woman, they're a poor idea for the woman who is trying to be appealing. Glasses make her more authoritative, and there is a direct reverse correlation between authority and appeal.

I advise women who wear glasses to wear contact lenses socially and to wear conventional glasses for business.[3]

In our interviewing, it was evident that women who are just entering the profession have not totally accepted the idea of the woman's business uniform. Phrases like "cookie cutter," "trying to fit in a mold," would crop up when talking about the subject of dress. It was almost as if they felt *different* by dressing in similar fashion. From the man's point of view, he has not lost his individuality, even though he dresses similarly to all his other professional companions.

Almost as an argument for the woman's uniform, Susan Butler related one of the dress problems women face. Included in her speech about executive women, she says,

"Hotel personnel can identify men executives by the way they dress. However, an executive who happens to be a woman has a problem, because not all women executives dress similarly, and hotel personnel cannot distinguish them from tourists or casual travelers. Therefore, women executives tend to receive different service, or different room assignments, and the quality of the services will differ from that given to men executives." In the final analysis, women should not feel defensive about their business uniform and are as entitled to their uniform as men professionals are to theirs. In fact, if women consistently adopted the uniform as their primary professional dress, certain benefits might accrue, such as being taken more seriously at first glance.

Black Women Accountants

The problems encountered by the black woman accountant are more numerous than those encountered by white women accountants, for the simple reason that she battles problems specific to her race in addition to all those shared by women in general. As shown in the following description of the entrance of black women into the profession, occasionally her color has worked to her advantage.

Black women have constituted a larger proportion of the black labor force than have all women of the total labor force since statistics began to be accumulated in 1890.[4] Further, more than half the black professionals since 1940 have been women. Accountants were placed in a separate category of the U.S. labor statistics in 1910, and at that time women constituted 20 percent of the black accountants. By 1950 that percentage had grown to 34 percent, and by 1970 to 45 percent. These statistics indicate that black women moved into the accounting profession, as a percentage of all black professionals, more quickly than white women.

However, blacks have never constituted a sizeable proportion of the public accounting profession. The large national firms did not begin to hire blacks until legislation that prohibited discriminatory hiring practices was enacted. Prior to the early 1970's black accountants were found only in local firms with black clientele. This was true of all the professions except teaching and nursing. These two have been dominated by women since the beginning of the century. Male-dominated professions, such as public accountancy, law, medicine, architecture, and engineering, were strictly segregated until legislative pressures began to open small cracks in their closed doors. But time produced change, and by 1981 such journals as *Essence,* a magazine published for contemporary black women, were reporting the opportunities available for black women in accounting.[5] There were a reported 1,400 black women accountants in the U.S. at that time, according to Benjamin Newhouse, the executive director of the National Association of Black Accountants.

In the early 1970's black women accountants with the professional training needed for public accounting were in very high demand, more so than black men. The larger accounting firms were under pressure to hire minorities, and a black woman covered two bases—she was both a woman and she was black. The graduate most in demand in 1973 was reported in *Money,* a professionally-oriented magazine, as a black woman with some kind of business or engineering degree.[6] That journal reported that two black women accountants who graduated near the top of the class that year from a university in the Southwest had no trouble getting better paying jobs than their classmates got. Both of them, one with a Master's and the other with a Bachelor's degree, received starting salaries considerably above the norm. The impact of anti-discriminatory hiring legislation was evident, for at that time starting salaries for women accounting graduates were 4 percent above those offered to men graduates.

The AICPA began their encouragement of the recruitment and hiring of blacks at the same time that they began to encourage the hiring of women. Their first effort came in 1969 through the formation of the Minority Recruitment and Equal Opportunity Committee. Since that time the AICPA has actively worked to get minorities to study accounting, and has disbursed millions of dollars to universities for accounting scholarships for black and Hispanic students. This effort continues today, and blacks with an interest in accounting as a career are usually able to secure some type of financial aid for their university study. Unfortunately the amounts are small, usually only enough to cover tuition and books at a public university. Room and board expenses must be met some other way. Needless to say, the scholarships are never enough to cover the tuition at a private university.

A study on the utilization of blacks by public accounting firms in Florida indicated that although women had been accepted for some time, the traditional objections still persisted for blacks.[7] The preponderance of firms in that state did not have blacks on their staffs. The reasons they gave for not having them were:

	Respondents	
	Number	**Percent**
None sought employment	37	49%
Interviewees were not as qualified as others	15	20%
Anticipated client resistance	15	20%
Anticipated staff resistance	8	11%
	75	100%

These are precisely the same reasons given a decade earlier for not hiring women, and they proved false in every respect. Today, in the mid-1980's, these same biased perceptions are beginning to crumble for blacks, but another decade may be required before anything close to full acceptance can be realized.

The few black women who have made it to the top in the large national firms are proving that black women are accepted by all types of clients, by staff at all levels, and that they are indeed highly qualified. Sheila Clark, a partner in the Houston office of the international firm of Peat, Marwick, Mitchell is one of these highly successful black women. She grew up in the Fifth Ward of Houston, a black inner-city area. While in high school she went to a career-day seminar and heard a presentation by one of the partners of a large national accounting firm, and she decided almost on the spot that she would give it a try. She remembers that in her first accounting course there were almost 250 students in the class, and she was one of two women in the group. She recalls vividly the words of her instructor after her first class when he told her the class was only for accounting majors; when she said she was one, he told her that she would quickly change her mind. But remarks like that only gave her stronger resolve; Sheila Clark said at that point she would have stuck it out no matter what, because she loves challenges.

When she received a bachelor's degree in accounting in 1969, with the profession hardly open to women, much less a black one, the only public accounting position she could find would have necessitated her going to Los Angeles or New York. She did not want to go that far from home, so she worked in industry in Houston for a year and then went back to school for a Master's degree. When she finished that degree in 1972, blacks were a bit more accepted in public accounting, and she took an offer from Peat, Marwick in Houston. Today Sheila Clark is an audit partner in the firm, specializing in government audits, which she readily admits she was channeled into, even though it is not considered as prestigious as some other areas. Her clients include the Houston School District, which has an annual budget of astronomical size.

She is very visible in the firm, in the profession, and in the community. This visibility places her in a position to convince everyone with whom she comes into contact that black women are the equal of anyone in the profession. They face double the problems which others have to face, being both women and black, but Sheila is an example of how one woman faced these problems and reached the top in a very demanding profession.

Career and Marriage

There are three key events that have led to the influx of women into the work force, all of which have occurred within the past ten to fifteen years. These three are economic necessity, search for personal fulfillment, and technological advances in "homemaking." Men and women alike are moving away from the traditional success ethic and more toward a "quality of life" ethic. Two incomes, whether a necessity for the couple or not, are one of the basic keys to new life/career choices.

Balancing career and marriage is probably the most common personal problem that women in public accounting face. The two-career family is now so commonplace that it is in many cases the expected role for well-educated couples. The widespread acceptance of dual careers is one of the strongest forces currently working to reduce sex-role stereotyping.

Dual-Career Problems

Young women who married prior to their entry into public accounting have the problem of adjusting their long overtime hours to the schedules of their husbands or families. This is especially true when the young accountant enters the profession as a married woman just out of college. Her adjustment and that of her family are particularly acute, because the wife's schedule is at the same time more demanding for her and more disruptive for the family. If the husband has a job with regular hours while she works overtime, a strain on their personal life is almost inevitable.

Stress resulting from work arrangements may not be as great in those cases where the couple meet, get to know each other, and marry while both are in public accounting. In these cases they are both attuned to long and somewhat irregular schedules, and they understand the necessity for it. The period prior to marriage permits each to become accustomed to the other's work requirements and the problems of being separated when one must travel out of town with the audit team. They both understand that clients and bosses can sometimes make unexpected demands upon them. There is stress, to be sure, but the likelihood is greater that it exists in an understanding environment.

Marriage of a public accountant to someone outside of public accounting presents a different set of problems. If the husband is a professional person, such as an attorney, the marital stress brought on by long overtime hours may be less, because he also experiences time demands and understands the necessity for them. Many of the women we interviewed were happily married to professional men; and though their lives were busy, they knew how to live it together. She was willing to put up with her husband's overtime, and he was willing to put up with hers. They indicated that frequent short vacations, sometimes no more than long weekends, gave them that necessary time together to keep the alliance on an even keel. Some adapted by taking separate vacations, since neither of them could seem to find a free week at the same time.

When the husband is not a professional person, there is a higher probability that their conflicting schedules will produce high levels of stress. Unless he is understanding and tolerant, such stress is fertile breeding ground for marital problems. The male with a strong indoctrination of the "appropriate" sex-roles may not be the best marital prospect for a woman who wants to be successful in public accounting. Long overtime hours, somewhat irregular schedules, and traveling with a team from the office for days or even weeks at a time are not conditions conducive to comfort for men with traditional sex role concepts.

Women in public accounting receive reasonably good salaries, and more and more cases are arising in which the wife's salary exceeds that of her husband. This presents a potentially abrasive problem, if the husband's self-esteem is low or if he is not receptive to equality of the sexes. One woman partner in a large national firm, who receives a substantial income, said, "It takes a strong man to handle this situation. I have not had a problem with my husband because we perceive our money as being a pool that we both use, and not 'her money' and 'his money.' We are involved in different lines of work, and he has chosen his work and I have chosen mine, and he sees advantages and disadvantages in his, as I do in mine. But we don't let money differences get in the way." She went on to comment that although her salary did not present a problem to her husband, it seemed to make a difference to some of their friends, especially couples where only the husband worked. She said that there were occasionally statements such as, "We can't afford that, but of course you and Bob can, because you both work." It is a two-edged sword—so many advantages and choices open up for the two-income family, but it also eliminates many opportunities (such as staying home with the children) available to those wives who don't work.

Successful Dual-Career Marriages

One study identified several common characteristics that a couple should have to improve the chances of a successful dual-career marriage. These were:

* Similar career stage needs. They should have similar needs to develop their personal skills and contacts.
* Ability to resolve conflicting career path alternatives. They should have the patience, understanding, and communication abilities which permit them to resolve conflicting career alternatives in a way that is satisfactory to both of them. When one has to sacrifice on the career ladder for the other it should be as much a compromise as possible.
* Equal commitment to career goals. They should be equally committed to their careers, and their commitment balance between family and career should be relatively equal. If one is committed to a career more than to family, and the other more to family than career, then resolving the conflicting career path alternatives will be extremely difficult.
* Informed about the other's work requirements and demands. Without information about the other there

is difficulty reaching decisions that are just and equitable when conflicts occur.
* Have equal resolve to approach their employer about possible solutions when conflicts arise. If one approaches her employer about possible solutions to a conflict, while the other is reluctant or refuses to do so, then equitable solutions may not be reached.
* Personal flexibility. This is an essential ingredient, and one which must be present to resolve the unknown and unexpected conflicts which arise when both spouses work.[8]

Whose Career Comes First?

The attitudes that grow from sex-role stereotyping have a strong impact upon how a married couple, both of whom are professionals, settle the frequently encountered problem of whose career will take precedence. Undoubtedly circumstances will arise when they must make decisions requiring that one of the two careers be given priority. An opportunity for advancement for one of them, requiring a relocation, is a common occurrence today. The relocation usually causes the other person to take a step backward in his or her career, or that it be abandoned altogether. On the other hand, rejection of the promotion and staying at the present location will mean that the career advancement of one is lessened in deference to the career of the other. The particular solution selected by the couple will depend almost directly upon their sex-role attitudes. And we must not forget that there is another solution—one goes and the other stays!

If the sex-role attitudes of both the husband and wife are those of a generation ago, that motherhood and being a wife constitute the "true" role of a woman, she may have no choice but to go or dissolve the marriage. If their values are those of a new, more liberated generation that accepts women as equals, an in-depth analysis of the situation, an investigation of alternate solutions, and a joint decision that keeps the marriage intact may be possible.

Career and Children

Since in public accounting the great majority of new staff and seniors are in their twenties, it is at this stage that marriages and the birth of children are more frequent. The problem of balancing family and career commitments thus is a problem faced by both women and men. One of the young women partners described the problem this way:

> I have noticed that when married men have families, their time commitment to work begins to cut back, but not quite as much as women when they have children. It is still easier for the male to say, "I can't come home until late tonight; I have to finish this project," and the next day he may leave at four in the afternoon because the project is finished and he wants to be with his family. But the woman who is on the same project may not be able to stay late because she has to pick up her child at the day care center before six in the evening. Both men and women feel the pressure of family commitments, but the woman feels it more.

REFERENCES

1. Schoof, C., "Women CPA's: A Status Report," *Outlook*, June, 1983, pp. 44–48.
2. Josefowitz, J., "Management Men and Women: Closed vs. Open Doors," *Harvard Business Review*, Vol. 58, No. 5, September/October, 1980, pp. 57–58.
3. Malloy, John, "The Women's Guide to Dressing for Success," *World*, Peat, Marwick, Mitchell & Co., Winter, 1978, pp. 43–48.
4. Kilson, M., "Black Women in the Professions," *Monthly Labor Review*, U.S. Department of Labor, Bureau of Labor Statistics, Vol. 100, No. 5, May, 1977, pp. 38–41.
5. "Accounting: Turning Over a New (Golden) Leaf," *Essence*, Vol. 2, No. 8, December, 1981, pp. 33–34.
6. "Token Women," *Money*, Vol. 2, No. 8, August, 1973, pp. 68–69.
7. Dennis, D. and Stephens, W., "Recruitment and Utilization of Minority Group Members by Florida CPA's," *Collected Papers of the AAA Southeast Regional Group*

27th Annual Meeting, Richmond, Virginia, April 24, 1975, pp. 121–123.

8. Hall, F., and Hall, D., "Dual Careers—How Do Couples and Companies Cope with the Problems," *Organizational Dynamics,* Vol. 6, No. 4, Spring, 1978, pp. 57–77.

Mutual Support and Visibility—Womens' Organizations

Organizations of persons with similar interests and goals provide a mechanism that not only reinforces individual commitments but provides a communication vehicle and a visible, united front. Naturally, men's accounting associations were the first to be formed in this country. In 1882 the Institute of Accountants and Bookkeepers, later known as the Institute of Accountants, was organized. Its purpose was to "foster the development of the profession through education." In 1887 the American Association of Public Accountants was formed, with its stated purpose being "to associate into a Society or Guild for mutual benefit and advantage, and through such association to elevate the profession of Accountancy as a whole."

These two associations joined forces to get the first certified public accountancy laws enacted, succeeding in New York in 1896 with the first licensing statute. Pennsylvania enacted similar legislation in 1899 authorizing the designation of CPA. Other states followed in quick succession.

American Women's Society of CPA's

Women's organizations appeared as soon as there was a nucleus of women CPA's available. That they organized early is no surprise, nor are the vigor and enthusiasm which their early founders exhibited. In 1933, when there were only 116 women CPA's in the nation out of a total of some 15,000, these few women felt the need for the individual and collective support that could be provided by an organization directed specifically to their needs. During the greatest depression ever to affect this nation, nine women met in Chicago for the specific purpose of forming some sort of coalition that would bring the few women in the profession together. They felt that they could know each other better, discuss mutual problems, and search for solutions to those problems more effectively through an organization of women CPA's. The American Women's Society of CPA's (AWSCPA) was born that year in the early spring of 1933.

Founders of the AWSCPA

The woman who was instrumental in forming the organization was Anna Francis. She shared her feelings with Grace Schwartz, and together they invited other women CPA's in the midwest area to the Chicago meeting held on January 4, 1933. Eight women attended that initial meeting; a ninth, Clara Stahl, supported the move but was unable to attend. These nine are considered to be the founding members of the organization.

Lee Ella Costella, president of the AWSCPA in 1957–58, commented on the nine who formed the organization in this way: "January, 1933, was perhaps one of the hardest periods of the Great Depression, and in many parts of the country a 'lady accountant' was just a dreamer, and a woman CPA was unheard of. Yet, there were actually more than a hundred women CPA's in the country, and nine of them had the courage and foresight to organize the American Women's Society of Certified Public Accountants. When I think of

Anna Grace Francis, Grace Schwartz Keats, Mary Gildea, Anna Lord, Adriana Van Kooy, Ruth Waschau, Georgia Davis, Josephine Kroll, and Clara Stahl, I think of the adjectives 'brave, steadfast, and unselfish,' because I know it was with no thought of gain for themselves they gave our Society its start, but I know they were inspired to take a daring step in the interest of other women accountants."

The enthusiasm of these nine was not short-lived. Fifty years later, in 1983, at the fiftieth year celebration of the founding of the AWSCPA, held in Chicago, two of these founding members were in attendance. The only other living member of the original nine was not there because of a confining illness. They were indeed dedicated women, with active participation spanning half a century.

The nine held CPA certificates from Illinois, Indiana, and Michigan, and they immediately began to contact other women CPA's. Invitations to join brought the total membership to twenty-six during the next six months, and then the first annual meeting was held that July in Chicago. That particular date and place was selected because the World's Fair was in progress in Chicago.

Response to the AWSCPA

Ten years later, in 1943, the membership had grown to 75, out of a total of 197 women CPA's in the nation. By 1953 the membership had grown to 294. Today the membership of the AWSCPA and its sister organization, the American Society of Women Accountants, approaches 5,000 dedicated women, and the rate of growth continues to accelerate.

Women in the early years of the organization were eager for an opportunity to associate with others who were experiencing the same set of problems. Margaret Lauer, president of the organization in 1964–65, expressed her memories of those days in this way:[1] "I had received my CPA certificate in 1932; I had been cordially accepted as a member of the Louisiana Society of CPA's shortly after its receipt; I had been politely interviewed by several CPA firms and received offers from two—each explaining that I could take charge of the office accounting, do some 'write-up work,' for clients, but under no circumstances could they promise anything more, as their clients would be opposed to a 'woman auditor.' I felt somewhat discouraged. I had been looking forward to a 'CPA career.' I wondered what other women CPA's did, and there were none in Louisiana I could consult with. Suddenly, I received a letter from Chicago—AWSCPA had been formed, so women CPA's were establishing a means of communication with each other. It was a great day for me. I sent in my application right away and my dues—$2 per year, they were. And never was money better spent, for that year and every year since."

The work climate for women during the early years of the organization is so foreign to that existing today that most of us have trouble even imagining it. The few women in the profession felt isolated and unwanted. Sally Czaja, a young manager in the consulting division of Arthur Andersen and Co. in Chicago and currently historian of the AWSCPA, researched the history of the organization and attempted to picture those early days for us in her remarks at the 50th Anniversary meeting of the organization.

> Our group's existence began in 1933 at the Women's Club in Chicago. Anna Francis, a CPA practicing in Chicago, thought it would be a good idea to have a professional organization for women accountants so they could meet and help each other. Those were the days when some male accountants said they would go out of business before they employed a woman. Some colleges would not even accept a woman into their accounting programs. One of our past presidents, Hazel Skog, wanted to become an accountant when she graduated from High School, but it was several years before she was able to locate a college in her area that would accept women students. Persistence was definitely necessary if a woman was to succeed in the accounting profession. In fact, another of our presidents, Ida Broo, worked two years without pay just to get experience which would qualify her to take the

CPA exam. She became interested in accounting when she was working as a stenographer and her employing company was purchased by another company. The new owners said that her duties would now include keeping the books. Ida said "I didn't know a book from a hole in the wall, but since my salary was to be raised from $18 to $20 per week, I decided that I could learn." She did, and by 1925 she had found a way to get the qualifying experience, had passed the CPA exam, and went on to become the first woman member of the Indiana CPA Society, and in 1950 the first woman member and president of a State Board of Accountancy.[2]

In spite of the need of these early women accountants for mutual support, acceptance into the organization in the early years was not automatic. The number of women CPA's was so small and the alliance so fragile that a single "trouble maker" or dissident member could seriously hurt the organization. Each prospective member was voted on individually by the entire membership after group discussion of her qualifications and her personality. Gertrude Priester, one of the early members, received her certificate in New York in 1934 and was voted on and admitted in 1935. During the discussion of her admittance she remembers sitting outside the room, waiting. She recalled that as she sat there she was dying for a cigarette, but was afraid that if she lit up and someone came out and saw her, they would not accept her. Smoking during those years was not as acceptable for women as it is today. She was admitted, of course, and later went on to be president of the organization from 1939 to 1941.

In 1937 the woman CPA was "one in a million." The members of AWSCPA proudly made that statement at their 1937 annual meeting, since there were approximately 125 to 130 women CPA's in the nation, and the population of the U.S. that year was 130 million. They were, indeed, one in a million.

Today local chapters of the women's organization exist in every large city, providing the mechanism for communication and personal interaction which did not exist in the early days. These local chapters meet monthly, and the annual convention is well attended. Publication of a monthly newsletter and a widely circulated professional journal, *The Woman CPA*, also provide a means by which women professional accountants are able to stay in touch with each other. This is indeed a far cry from the isolation which these early women professionals felt.

The three primary objectives of the AWSCPA, now as in the early years, are:[3]

> *Encouragement of women accountants in their professional advancement.
> *Improvement of knowledge within the accounting profession concerning the ability and achievements of women CPA's.
> *Increase in the number of women who are members and active participants in programs of technical accounting organizations.

Early Leaders of AWSCPA

The early women leaders of the organization were, in comparison to other professional societies, a very unselfish group. The comments of Lee Ella Costella which were given earlier in this chapter and described this rather admirable trait, were further confirmed by Marie Dubke, president of AWSCPA in 1968–69. Commenting on her term of office, she described in this way the people in the organization who touched her life:

> Francis Britt, president 1967–68, was so modest and unpretentious. She was the one who got us to have the current officers preside at the annual meetings. Up until then we aped the AICPA (men's organization) and had the one who went out of office last June preside at an October meeting. What confusion. We had four presidents to sort out. It was hard to tell the players even with the program. She never presided, because she skipped the glory and made me preside instead, to get us on the new schedule. She was a real gem, and did much for the organization.

Margaret Lauer, president 1964–65, is another diamond. She is above all the most perfect lady there is in AWSCPA. Her method of gently reasoning together has solved many a problem for the society.

Ula Motekat—our diamond in the rough. She was opposed by many who did not want her to be editor. We were afraid that she was too 'women's lib,' but she turned the magazine into a journal, and it has grown in stature. The work was started earlier by Mary Hall and Mary Jo McCann. Mary Hall got us into a more modern-looking format, and it was Phyllis Peters who insisted that we would be proud of Ula. She was so right.[4]

The AWSCPA held a twenty-fifth year celebration in New York in 1958. Five of the nine founding members were in attendance and were still active. The membership was relatively small, since the profession had not yet opened its doors to women; it boasted a total membership of 400, with members from some 40 states. The organization had elected a total of twenty presidents during these twenty-five years, five of them serving double terms. These women were highlighted in the program booklet from the twenty-fifty year celebration. Some of the honors and recognitions given to them at that time are listed here.[5]

1933–35.   Anna G. Francis, CPA. Practiced public accounting in Chicago, where she also taught bookkeeping, accounting, and commercial law. She was a primary figure in organizing the AWSCPA.

1936–37.   Anne M. Lord, CPA. She practiced in her own name in Aurora, Illinois. She holds the B.A. in mathematics from Smith College, and is a board member, officer, and trustee of many philanthropic organizations.

1937–39.   Ruth Peabody Waschau, CPA. Controller of National Engineering Company, Chicago. She has both a B.S. and an M.S. in Accountancy from the University of Illinois and obtained her experience with Haskins and Sells.

1939–41.   Gertrude Priester, CPA. She is a graduate of New York University with a BSC in Accounting, has been a director of the Committee on Women in World Affairs and served on several committees of the New York State Society of CPA's.

1941–42. Ida S. Broo, CPA. She practices in her own name in Indianapolis, Indiana. She was a member of the Indiana State Board of Accountancy for six years, serving as president for two years.

1942–43. Grace A. Dimmer, CPA. She is a partner in the firm of Shaw, Olsen & Dimmer, located in Detroit. Active as officer in the Michigan Association of CPA's and serving on significant committees of the American Institute of CPA's.

1943–44. Grace S. Keats, CPA. In practice with her father, following graduation from Northwestern University, in the firm name of G. W. Schwartz and Daughter, CPA's.

1944–45. Hazel J. Skog, CPA. Practices in her own name in Spokane, Washington. A graduate of Kinman Business College, she has served as vice-president, president, and as representative of the Spokane Chapter of CPA's to the Washington State Board of Public Accountancy.

1946–46. Ethleen Lasseter, CPA. She is an assistant trust officer of the First National Bank of Atlanta, Georgia. She served as editor of *The Woman CPA* and was a frequent contributor to that journal.

1946–47. Jennie M. Palen, CPA. Formerly with Haskins and Sells, she is now instructor of accountancy at the City College of New York and is a distinguished poet and author.

1947–48. Heloise Brown Canter, CPA. She practices in her own name in Houston, Texas. A graduate of Mary Hardin Baylor College, she was an official delegate of the AICPA to the First Inter-American Conference on Accounting in San Juan.

1948–49. Ruth A. Clark, CPA. She is treasurer and assistant secretary of Lyon Van & Storage in Los Angeles. She attended Indiana State Teachers College and has served as chairperson of a number of committees of the Los Angeles chapter of CPA's.

1949–50. Marion A. Frye, CPA. She practices public accounting under her own name in Cleveland, with branch offices in several other Ohio cities. She was an official delegate of the AICPA to the third annual Inter-American Conference on Accounting in Sao Paulo, Brazil.

1950–51. Edith Moore, CPA. She is with the firm of J. H. Hardy & Associates in Chattanooga, Tennessee, and has served on committees and as secretary of the Chattanooga Chapter of CPA's.

1951–52. Jean D. Colavecchio, CPA. She is a supervisor in the tax department of Ernst & Ernst in Providence, Rhode Island. She graduated from Northeastern University and is Secretary and Director of the Rhode Island Society of CPA's.

1952–53.   Helen F. McGillicuddy, CPA and LLB. She currently practices law and accountancy in Chicago and is lecturer in Accounting at Northwestern University.

1953–54.   Rosemary Hoban, CPA. She is a supervisor in the tax department of Touche Niven, Bailey and Smart in Detroit, where she has served on committees of the Michigan Association of CPA's.

1954–55.   Elinor Hill, CPA. She is a partner in the firm of H. B. Richardson & Co., in Passaic, New Jersey. She graduated from Rutgers and is an active participant in civic and philanthropic organizations.

1955–56.   Corinne Childs, CPA and LLB. She practices in her own name in Tulsa, Oklahoma. She is serving her fourth year on the editorial advisory board of *The Journal of Accountancy*.

1956–57.   Elizabeth A. Sterling, CPA. She is a partner with her husband in Atlanta, Georgia. She graduated from Georgia State University and has served as a trustee for the Georgia State Society of CPA's.

These women have received many appointments and recognitions since the 1958 meeting which honored them, but only those recognitions received prior to that meeting are described here. There is no question that they took their responsibilities as leading officers of the AWSCPA seriously. Margaret Lauer, president in 1965–66, commented on her presiding at the 1965 convention in Dallas with these memories: "I very nearly came to missing it entirely. Just the week before, New Orleans was visited by Betsy, the worst hurricane since 1915. The city was a shambles, my home likewise. It was still standing, but the roof was practically gone, and the deluge of water which poured in ruined not only personal belongings but, worst of all, some printed matter prepared for the meeting and all of my typed procedures, speeches and all. The accommodating printer, working by candlelight and using a handpress (electricity was nonexistent), replaced the printing. With the help of my secretary, Beryl Doherty, who obligingly went to Dallas with me, the typed matter was redone, and the meeting proceeded smoothly, those in attendance unaware that everything presented by me was hot off the griddle."

Accomplishments of the AWSCPA

One of the first organized efforts of the AWSCPA was to gather data concerning the general demographics of women CPA's in the U.S. They immediately went to work to gather information from every woman CPA they could locate. These surveys continue to be taken today and provide valuable information. This first effort, however provided an invaluable data base and a point of comparison for all the later efforts. On February 11, 1935, the results of the first survey were released. A total of 105 women CPA's were located and contacted, and of these only thirty-seven were in public practice—seventeen practicing in her own name, eight practicing in partnerships, and twelve employed by others. Five women CPA's were employed as Internal Revenue auditors, and two were teaching accounting at women's colleges. One, Clara Stahl, had received a silver medal from the State of Illinois for the second highest scores on the CPA exam given in that state.

The original survey, as well as those which followed, indicated that the women who joined the organization were active leaders in other groups also. A pamphlet entitled *Women Certified Public Accountants—1956,* which was published by the educational committee of the AWSCPA, stated that 25 percent of the women responding to the survey reported participating in other professional accounting organizations as committee members, committee chairpersons, officers, or directors.[6]

The 1956 pamphlet also disclosed that 6 percent of those in the survey were employed in government positions requiring accounting training. To provide more opportunities for women in government where a shortage of Certified Public Accountants existed, the Legislative Committee of the organization endeavored to eliminate discrimination against the employment of women accountants in various federal agencies. One result was the lifting of the blanket restriction against the employment of women accountants in the General Accounting Office (GOA). The committee, acting jointly with the ASWA Legislative Committee, induced Congresswoman Marguerite S. Church of Illinois to introduce H.R. 2858, a bill to amend Section 33, Title V, of the United States Code which would eliminate the right of appointing officers to specify the sex of the persons given appointments to government positions. This type of action reflects the results of the concerted and organized efforts of the AWSCPA.

Annual meetings of the society have been held since the first one in 1933. Their programs include educational seminars, business meetings, social events, professional papers, and, as is common for professional societies, sightseeing and enjoying the local ambience. Marie Dubke described how she benefited from these meetings in this way: "I missed one meeting because I did not believe I could afford it. Little did I know that the cost spent is amply returned in new knowledge and inspiration. It is a chance to plug in and get recharged for another year of new goals and accomplishments. Through the annual meetings, I met such super friends. Perhaps the one who made the greatest impression on me was Gertrude Priester—I was young enough at first that I could literally sit at her feet at conventions and hear about the old days and the times of real trial and tribulation."

Presiding at the annual meetings was sometimes a touchy business. Since women were not yet accepted into the profession, unexpected surprises could arise. In 1960 Kay Pfeifer was the president, presiding at the annual meeting in Philadelphia. The organization had invited the then president of AICPA to speak at their banquet. He presented a speech written for him by the AICPA staff which he had not read prior to the meeting. It was an insulting speech, questioning the purpose of the women's organization and asking why it did not disband! Kay, as president, took the stand following that speech. She was a tiny woman, and needed a box to reach the podium. She answered his speech point by point, even though she had to extemporize, and did it in such a low-key way that AWSCPA came out appearing as gracious hostesses not to be put down by male chauvinists. She died not too long afterward, but she will be remembered for her quick wit, sharp mind, and the courage to stand for her convictions.

In 1965 the AWSCPA established its Educational Foundation. The foundation was inspired by a bequest from Anna Grace Francis, the first president of the organization. During those years the organization was printing and distributing large quantities of educational, promotional, and career materials, the cost of which was draining its financial resources. Thus the AWSCPA board agreed to restrict the bequest of Anna Grace Francis until a foundation could be formed that would be dedicated to education. Contributions are received today from members and outside contributors, and the fund continues to serve educational purposes. This educational foundation sponsors national management seminars twice each year, in addition to career development activities, university scholarships for deserving women students, and sponsorship of student chapters at a number of universities.

In 1978 the Laurels Fund was established in memory of past president Sally Self (1974–75). The purpose of this fund was to recognize her contributions to the profession and to the organization. Today it utilizes its resources to provide scholarships to assist women seeking advanced degrees in accounting.

American Society of Women Accountants

During the early years of the AWSCPA there were so few women CPA's that even the larger cities were hard pressed to locate a sufficient number to have successful local chapters. There were a number of women accountants in these cities, but not enough were certified to provide the critical mass necessary for a successful professional society. Only

Chicago and New York were able to maintain active chapters of the AWSCPA, although there were members scattered in every large city in the nation. According to informal estimates, there were in 1937 about 17,000 in the U.S. performing accounting work who had not passed the CPA exam. Although many were just accounting clerks, an equal number of these women held very responsible positions, and Ida Broo, a member of ASWCPA, felt that they, too, needed an organization to provide mutual support and interaction. She recognized that a coalition of certified and non-certified women accountants could provide the necessary numbers for successful intercity organization.

Ida began by selling other members of the AWSCPA on the need for an auxiliary organization. She was appointed as chairperson of a planning committee, with Charlotte Liszt, Ruth Peabody Waschau, and Anne Lord completing the committee. Ida, in a subsequent report to the AWSCPA, stated that she and two other women sat on her back porch in May 1938, and laid the plans for the new organization. Ida lived in Indianapolis, and in June, ten women from that city met for the first meeting. Twenty-seven others applied for membership the next month, and by the end of August, a total of sixty had joined. Ida then submitted the proposed constitution and bylaws of the new organization to the board of directors of the AWSCPA for approval.

Thus the American Society of Women Accountants (ASWA) was given life. The first chapter was followed in quick succession by chapters in Chicago, New York, Spokane, and Detroit. Within a short time there were chapters in 120 cities throughout the nation. Incidentally, this organization is open to men, although few have joined.

For the record, the original name proposed for this new professional society was the American Woman's Society of Junior Accountants. Fortunately, this name was not chosen, and the more professional name currently used was adopted.

Up to 1938, all of the annual meetings of the parent organization had been held in Chicago, primarily because of its geographical location. With the new group of women now available as a result of the formation of the ASWA, and because the World's Fair was being held there, the 1939 meeting was shifted to New York City. During the course of the meeting a telegram was received which reported the official formation of a new chapter in Spokane, Washington. Ida, with her characteristic sense of humor, reported the event and said, "Now, girls, we are coast to coast without counting stops in between."

The sixth chapter of the ASWA was a student chapter. By the middle of 1940, the women students at Temple University in Philadelphia had become upset over the discriminatory conditions they were encountering. One university in that area had refused to admit women to day classes in accounting, while another had denied them membership in the honorary student accounting fraternity, even though they had met the scholastic requirements. The five students met at the Arcadia Restaurant with the presidents of AWSCPA and ASWA to learn of the purposes of the organizations. As a result of this meeting, the Philadelphia chapter was formed with the five students as charter members. It quickly grew to be one of the larger chapters.

In 1943 the public relations committees of the two organizations petitioned Beta Alpha Psi, the honorary accounting fraternity, to open its membership to women. Their request for action was acknowledged by the National President of Beta Alpha Psi, who said that the matter would be submitted to the grand council, which would probably not meet that year. The women also put pressure on John Carey, executive director of the AICPA, to have membership in Beta Alpha Psi opened to women. John Carey replied that he might "find an appropriate opportunity to drop a helpful word on the subject." In spite of this foot-dragging, the honorary fraternity was eventually opened to women, due largely to the pressures of the two women's organizations.

Through the years the ASWA has held steadfastly to its stated purposes—to increase the interest of women in the accounting profession, to increase the opportunities for women in accounting, and to inform the public of the place women hold in the field. Its membership is open to practicing accountants and to teachers of accounting who have two years of practical experience. If a member passes the CPA exam, she is eligible for membership in the AWSCPA also. The organization shares in the educational foundation of the AWSCPA.

The somewhat unusual relationship between the AWSCPA and ASWA caught the attention of the older and larger, male-dominated American Institute of CPA's. They had long been concerned with the lack of interface between CPA's and non-certified accountants who were not in public practice. The arrangement worked out by the women prompted a comment in an AICPA board meeting in 1947, but no follow-through was undertaken by that board to effect a similar arrangement. After all, the critical mass for organizational purposes existed for the men, since there were plenty of male CPA's, and such an alliance was not of immediate nor direct value to the male-dominated AICPA.

In 1946 the officers of the women's organizations decided that the annual meetings should be held two days preceding, and in the same location as, the male-dominated AICPA. Thus the AWSCPA members could stay for the national meeting of the AICPA if they chose. The AICPA welcomed the women and even introduced the president of the AWSCPA from the floor, but then voted to have its meeting the next year in Miami, Florida, which was then about as out-of-the-way as possible for a national organization. Deciding that a more central location would be better for them, the women selected Grand Rapids as their meeting site. However, the custom of meeting at the same place as the AICPA was resumed the next year and has been followed every year since, except for one year. In 1981 the women did not meet in Chicago, where the AICPA had its meeting, choosing instead to boycott Chicago to show displeasure with non-passage of the Equal Rights Amendment by the Illinois legislature. They met instead in Memphis.

Women's Professional Publications

Perhaps the most visible aspect of the AWSCPA is its professional journal, *The Woman CPA*. This journal provides a means of communication between women CPA's, but perhaps its most valuable contribution is in calling attention to the professional activities and the professionalism of women CPA's. During the early years of the organization the need for a monthly newsletter was strong, and the journal evolved from such a newsletter. In 1937 the first mimeographed bulletin was issued, and at that point it contained both news of a personal nature and material of a professional nature. Since membership was less than 100, personal news was well received. As the organization grew, so did the need for more professional recognition. Within a few years the organization needed a more extensive and more professional organ. In 1943 the bulletin became a professional journal and was given the title *The Woman CPA*.

At that time, longer articles of professional quality were published along with more advertising. The format was similar to that of other professional journals of the era; in 1974 it received a second face-lift to keep pace with similar journals. It is now a slick, polished professional journal of first-class appearance, with highly qualified professional editorial staffing and an elite editorial board.

The journal, issued quarterly, is the official publication of both the AWSCPA and the ASWA. It has been issued continuously since 1937. Libraries shelve the 1984 issue as Volume 46, one volume for each year of its existence. It is not a "woman's magazine," nor are the articles restricted to subjects of interest only to women. However, the editors do appear to have a preference for professional and technical articles written by women, especially if the woman is a member of the AWSCPA. In addition, since there is a backlog of good professional articles available for publication, women authors are given first preference.

A recent issue of the journal, selected at random from the

shelf of the library of the University of Houston, contained the following Table of Contents:[7]

* *Editorial*
    Philosophy and Change

* *Feature Articles*
    Depreciation and Landscaping
    Relations with State Society Members not in Public Accounting
    The Auditor's Independence Problem
    Medical Expense Deductions

* *Departments*
    Tax: Real Property Investment Decisions—ACRS vs. Straight Line Depreciation
    Electronic Data Processing: Some Behavioral Issues
    Non Business Organizations: Federal Grants— The Single Audit Concept

Obviously, a professional journal cannot serve well as both a professional vehicle and as a newsletter. Newsletters need a personal touch, and the information they convey is less technical in nature. To satisfy the need for the personal touch which was lost as the journal became more professional, the AWSCPA newsletter was reinstituted in 1955 as a monthly publication. It was entitled the *AWSCPA News* and became the official vehicle to inform members of significant events in the accounting profession, events in the women's movement, committee activities, cooperative projects with ASWA, and the activities and achievements of members. Elizabeth Sterling was the first editor of the newly constituted newsletter. So many requests were received from members during succeeding years that in 1973 the newsletter began to publish notices of career opportunities for women in the profession.

The ASWA *Coordinator* is the official monthly publication of that organization, serving as its newsletter.

Gatherings of Partners

Concurrent with the fiftieth year celebration of the AWSCPA in 1983, then-president Shirley Dahl, a partner in the Los Angeles office of Price Waterhouse, called a meeting of all women partners of large international firms. At that time, there were only sixty-eight women partners in the largest nine firms in the U.S., and twenty-six of them attended this first meeting, held in Chicago. It was an informal session, not intended as an organizational meeting to structure a formal entity—it was a meeting of women professionals with a rather unique set of common circumstances. Partnership for a woman in these large firms had been up to that time (and continues today, as described in an earlier chapter) a very difficult accomplishment. As a result, these women had a common experience and a more strongly felt need for mutual association. Some of the women partners in these large firms believe that should the number of women partners in Big Eight or Big Nine firms grow significantly, a suborganization within the AWSCPA may emerge.

In 1984 an attempt was made to establish an informal organization of women partners in large international firms in and around the New York City area. Susan Butler, a partner with Arthur Andersen in New York City, arranged a meeting of those women partners in the area. Although there are only twenty or so in the area, a dozen of these attended the first informal meeting. Their purpose, as stated by Susan Butler, was "to get to know each other better and to find ways to make ourselves, as women partners, more known and more visible."

Women professionals have an innate desire to be known as professionals and to be a recognized part of their chosen profession. They had to assert their rights to a place in the profession. Their organizations served them well in providing the visibility so greatly deserved, especially during the decades of the 1930's, 1940's, and 1950's. The needs served by these organizations today are not the same as were the needs served twenty years ago, but the organizations are now institutionalized and continue to be a viable force in the professional lives of their members.

REFERENCES

1. American Women's Society of CPAs, *Celebrating Our Past, Present, and Future,* Chicago, 1983.
2. Unpublished speech by Sally Czaja, written by Sally Czaja and Mary Moore, presented at the fiftieth anniversary meeting of the AWSCPA in Chicago, 1983.
3. American Women's Society of CPAs, *Women Certified Public Accountants,* Chicago, 1956.
4. *Celebrating Our Past, Present, and Future,* op. cit.
5. American Women's Society of CPAs, *Introducing Women Accountants, Past, Present, and Future,* Chicago, 1958.
6. American Women's Society of CPAs, *Women Certified Public Accountants,* Chicago, 1956.
7. *The Woman CPA,* Vol. 45, No. 4., October, 1983.

Women Public Accountants in Other Countries

Only a few countries in the world have public accounting professions that are as developed or as respected as in the United States. Similarly, the U.S. is ahead of or at least equal to every other country in the world in the acceptance of women into the public accounting profession. For that matter only a few cultures have an appreciable number of women in any of the recognized professions or in managerial positions which carry any significant degree of responsibility. Many countries have a high proportion of women in the work force, but this is a far cry from the acceptance of them into management. The developing countries and the nonindustrialized countries utilize women in large numbers, but they generally perform nonsupervisory tasks; in these countries a woman in a responsible managerial position or in one of the recognized professions would be a rarity indeed.

Only in industrialized countries that utilize free enterprise systems is the public accounting profession, as we know it, an indispensable cog in the wheels of commerce. A highly controlled economic system similar to those that

exist in Russia or China would have little need for independent auditors or tax advisors; management consulting is
assigned to government agencies. Public accountants, offering expertise in tax or management consulting and acting as
independent auditors, are needed only in those countries
where there exists free enterprise and established public
ownership of businesses. Free enterprise in an industrialized country fosters and encourages the formation of
new business with funds that are gathered from private
citizens through the issuance of stock, and these ownership
shares are traded freely in organized stock markets. For
these reasons comparisons of women in managerial positions, and certainly within the public accounting profession,
can be made in a meaningful way only for the industrialized
countries of the world.

Some additional insight into the place which women hold
in industrialized free enterprise countries can be obtained
from statistics gathered by the Institute of Personnel Management, located at Ashridge Management College in
London. They released the following table which reflects the
percentage of women administrators and managers in selected countries.[1]

**WOMEN AS A PERCENTAGE OF ADMINISTRATORS AND
MANAGERIAL WORKERS IN SELECTED COUNTRIES**

Country	Year	Percentage
Germany, Federal Republic	1978	15.6
Norway	1978	14.6
Spain	1978	1.5
Sweden	1975	11.4
United Kingdom	1979	16.3
United States	1978	23.5

Data were not available for exactly the same years for
each of the countries included in the study, but the dates are
close enough to provide comparisons. The U.S. had by far
the highest percentage of women in managerial positions,
with the United Kingdom and the Federal Republic of Germany a distant second and third. Spain, having a much more

male-dominated culture, has very few women in management.

The type of work done by public accountants, the laws governing the public accounting profession, and the general esteem that the public has for the profession differ greatly from one country to another, making these sorts of comparisons difficult. The following statistics were prepared by The Research Committee of the Los Angeles Chapter of the American Society of Women Accountants and reflect comparative data as of 1970.[2] Statistics such as these are not available for later years, and these data must be interpreted in light of the nature of public accounting in each country.

Number of Women "Certified" in 1970

Argentina (Buenos Aires)	1,384
Australia	40
Austria	64
Belgium	15
Denmark	4
France	98
Great Britain	625
Guatemala	7
Israel	26
Japan	26
Mexico	33
Netherlands	12
New Zealand	193
South Africa	20
Sweden	7
Thailand	1,012
United States	2,500

Argentina

Argentina appears to have a large number of women certified public accountants. The numbers are deceptive, however, because in most of the South American countries graduation from a university with an accounting degree is sufficient to register the graduate as a public accountant. The examinations that must be passed are all part of the university program and no experience requirements exist. In the Federal District of Buenos Aires, one of the most populous and most industrialized cities in South America, 15,000 students were studying accounting at the Argentine National University at the time these statistics were gathered, 30 percent of them women. Due to a high attrition and drop-out rate, only 400 or so are actually graduated each year; nevertheless, a large number of women in Argentina receive the degree and become "certified." Thus, by 1970, 1,384 women graduates had attained the title of Certified Public Accountant, although very few were in public practice, probably less than 100. There are no known statistics on how many were actually in practice.

Other South American Countries

In other South American countries the situation is similar to that in Argentina. Brazil also has an arrangement wherein the certification and university degree are awarded concurrently. There were no women known to be practicing public accounting in Brazil at the time of this study, although the number with "certificates" must have been relatively large. Uruguay is another country with this type of arrangement. In 1970 a total of 900 students had been graduated from its universities, receiving the certificate and degree, but only three women were active in public accounting at the time of this study. In Venezuela at that time, there were no laws governing the accounting profession, so anyone might assume the designation of public accountant. Mexico, on the other hand, has laws and regulations similar to those in the U.S., and there were in 1970 only thirty-three women who held the title "Contador Publico."

South American countries are not generally known for their liberal attitudes toward women. Accountancy in that area of the world is not highly regarded and is generally considered a quasi-clerical activity. The economies of most of the countries in South and Central American have not developed a high degree of industrialization, the public issuance of stocks and bonds is almost non-existent, and organized stock markets do not exist. Thus the services of public accountants, as auditors, tax advisors, and management consultants are not in high demand. As a result of these conditions, those women who study accounting and graduate with a "certificate" take positions as bookkeepers or accounting clerks. Those who are certified and actually work as public accountants are few in number.

Australia and New Zealand

Australia and New Zealand have formal educational and experience requirements similar to those for certification in the United States. Universities offer formal programs which train new entrants for the profession, and both experience as well as success on the professional examination are necessary before one becomes a Certified Public Accountant. At the time of this study only forty women public accountants in Australia were certified and actively engaged in the profession. Most of these were employees of firms owned by men public accountants. New Zealand had 193 women members of their Society of Accountants, but no data are available on how many of these were certified or in public practice.

Japan and Hong Kong

Japan is another country where the acceptance of women into business and the professions has been slow in coming. At the time of this study twenty-six women were certified out of a total of 4,480 Certified Public Accountants. No information is available on how many of these were in public practice. Japan not only offers training in accounting at the university level, but has an intermediate examination that precedes the certification examination. This examination is known as the "Junior CPA" examination and is an effective weeding-out step in the certification process.

Although a large number of women are involved in the lower levels of accounting work in Hong Kong, the Hong

Kong Association of Chartered Accountants did not in 1970 include any women members. It is not possible to attain the status of Certified Public Accountant in Hong Kong itself. In order to qualify for the title, a person must study in the United States or England. Accountancy is offered in technical schools and universities, but graduates must take positions in industry, commerce, or government, since public accountancy is not available to them. These programs of accounting study are available to women, but information on the male/female proportion was not available.

Thailand

Thailand presents a contrast to the industrialized countries of the western world. Accounting is taught in both government and private universities in a manner similar to that in South American countries, wherein the university degree and "certification" are practically concurrent. By 1970 a total of 1,012 licenses had been issued to women graduates. It is interesting to note that most of the students in the accountancy program of Chulolongkorn University, the largest public university in the country, are women. In a recent graduating class of 115 persons, only nine were men. One can speculate that in a country with the degree of industrialization that Thailand currently has, only limited need exists for public auditors, tax advisors, and management consultants as we know them. Thus most of the individuals who are "certified" are undoubtedly engaged in bookkeeping or clerical accounting tasks. Accountancy in Thailand appears to be one of the areas which, like nursing and primary school teaching, is a "woman's area."

South Africa

The only African country included in this study was South Africa. Most of the African countries have not reached a point where public accountancy is a viable profession. However, South Africa has university programs in accounting, and by 1970 twenty women had passed the professional examination. How many of these were in public practice is not known.

European Countries

Some of the European countries have several different certifications. Austria, as an example, has one group certified as auditors and a second group certified as tax advisors. There were sixty-four women in the two groups combined, of which sixty-three were in public practice.

Several of the European countries did not have formally structured public accounting professions as late as 1970. Portugal and Italy are examples. In Portugal, a university graduate in economics or law simply registers as a "technico de contos" with the Minister of Finance and thereby is authorized to certify to the accuracy of a company's financial affairs. The arrangement in Italy is somewhat similar. The "Ragioneris" or "Dottori Commercialisti" is a university graduate who, after registering with the Minister of Justice, may undertake the function of auditor. No examination is given to insure that the individual is qualified or has any understanding of auditing or accounting principles. It is little wonder that accounting work is not held in high regard in those countries and that "audited" financial statements continue to lack credibility.

The more industrialized European countries such as England, Germany, France, and Switzerland have well established and well respected accounting and auditing professions. Some of these countries utilize an apprenticeship requirement prior to entrance into the profession. This presents an additional barrier to the entrance of women into the public accounting profession. A training contract, or articled clerkship, must be agreed upon between a certified practitioner and the apprentice. There is reason to believe that in male dominated professions the acceptance of a woman apprentice would be resisted, and thus the entrance of women into the profession would be delayed. Great Britain and France are examples of countries that utilize an apprenticeship system.

At the time of this study the Institute of Chartered Accountants of England and Wales estimated that there were about 625 women members of the Institute out of a total membership of 45,500 public accountants. Of these, approximately 125 women were in public practice and another eighty were employed in the profession. The balance must have been in commerce, education, or government positions. A year or so prior to this study there were 3,850 articled-clerk registrations, of which only 184 were women.

We wish to emphasize that the statistics presented above were gathered in 1970, when women were just beginning to be accepted into the profession in the U.S. The industrialized countries of Europe were in a similar position relative to their acceptance of women. Today there is evidence that they have opened the doors of their recognized professions to women in a fashion similar to that which occurred in the U.S. since the early years of the 1970's.

Opening of the Profession in England

In order to provide a contrast between the U.S. and the industrialized European countries, the history of the opening of the profession to women in England is described below in some detail. There are striking similarities between the two countries. The first formal entrance of women into the profession in England came in 1920, in almost direct response to the passage of the Sex Disqualification Act of 1919. This law prohibited sex discrimination. Miss Mary Harris Smith had first requested admittance to the Institute of Chartered Accountants as early as 1891, but her application was denied.[3] Such a request was tantamount to an application to take the qualifying exam for a certificate as a Chartered Accountant. The use of exams was relatively new, and she had been in practice for over a decade.

She was not admitted until 1920, when the Sex Disqualification Act finally convinced the all-male organizations that they could no longer keep her out. At that time she was given the license of a Chartered Accountant without having to take an examination. The avowed reason for waiving the exam was her long decades of public practice. There is also reason to believe that the denial of permission to take the exam for almost three decades also had a bearing on the decision to waive it!

Mary Smith's original application for membership in 1891 was rejected following a ruling by the society that its bylaws contained only the words "he" and "his," which clearly ruled out the membership of women. At that time, almost one hundred years ago, it was socially unacceptable for an educated woman in England to work for a living. Miss Mary Harris Smith was an exception, a pioneer to whom women accountants in England owe a great deal. She was born in 1847, the daughter of a banker who recognized and encouraged her abilities with numbers and mathematical logic. Her father and his friends would entertain themselves and her by giving her difficult number problems to solve, which she did with great ability.

At the age of sixteen, she went to study mathematics at King's College, where she outshone her classmates. She went to work as an accountant in the offices of a private business. In 1878 she began to build up her own clientele and establish a public accounting practice. She had to build her public accounting business "on the quiet" for, as she expressed it, "my parents wish that the matter not be talked about in our own immediate circle."

Miss Smith had been practicing in public accounting for almost thirteen years before her initial unsuccessful application for membership in the professional society and the title of Chartered Accountant. She applied again in 1899. She had learned that the Royal Institute of British Architects had elected a woman to membership, even though their bylaws also contained only the words "he" and "his." But again she was rejected. There is a historical record which indicates that the president of the Institute stated, as a result of her second application, that, "It would be so embarrassing to manage a staff composed partly of women that he would rather retire from the profession than contemplate such a position."

Five years after Miss Smith broke the barrier and gained

admittance in 1920 there were only five women chartered accountants. The number increased very slowly for the next fifty years. The following table shows the number of women who were chartered in England since that first one in 1920.[4]

WOMEN MEMBERS OF THE INSTITUTE OF CHARTERED ACCOUNTANTS

Year	Number of Women
1920	1
1925	5
1930	32
1935	57
1940	84
1945	105
1950	137
1955	182
1960	342
1965	464
1970	711
1975	1,413
1976	1,608
1977	1,868

The chart is dated at intervals of five-year periods, except for the final three years. Note that only one year separates the period 1975–1977, when a very rapid growth in numbers occurred. In a fashion comparable to that which occurred in the United States, the rate of growth in England has accelerated during the past ten years.

A discussion of the entrance of women into the profession in England would be incomplete without a profile of Ethel Watts, one of the true pioneer women. She was the first woman to be admitted to the Institute of Chartered Accountants by way of examination, and in 1924 became its second woman member, following Miss Harris. She received an arts degree, and also served a full apprenticeship, having been articled to Mr. S. Williams, FCA. Why she chose accounting as a career is not known, but what is known is the resounding success she made of her career at a time and a place when women professionals were not only a rarity but also a curiosity.

Miss Watts joined the firm of Peats after becoming chartered, and there were many who questioned the firm's judgment in taking on a woman. She related later in her life that while with the firm she was not allowed even to answer the phone when a client called. Instead, a man would answer, relay the question to her, and return her answer to the client. This was undoubtedly a bit hard to take—so she started her own firm in 1925 under the name of Homersham & Watts. She later formed a single proprietorship, E. Watts & Co., with offices in Southwest London. She was active in the profession, serving on a number of significant committees of the Institute, and eventually served on the executive committee of the Institute's Benevolent Fund.

Miss Watts was unable to attend a number of the functions and dinners of the Institute and its local society during her early years as a member because they were held at clubs and restaurants that did not admit women. She replied after one such occasion to Ernest Whinney, who was chairman at the time, that she would have been welcome as a waitress, but not as a diner. Shortly afterwards the organization changed its meeting place to one that accepted women!

In 1945, when the number of women in the Institute was increasing, she formed the Women's Chartered Accountants' Dining Society, which continues today. The purpose of the organization was to provide an opportunity to meet, become acquainted, and share common interests. It was this group which founded and funded the award given today as the Ethel Watts Prize for achievement on the qualifying examinations. This award is internationally known and has been a fitting tribute to her memory.

Ethel Watts retired from practice in 1961. In an article describing her contributions, the following quote gives a graphic picture of her person:

> Life cannot have been easy for a woman in practice
> on her own at a time when women were not generally

accepted in the professions. She must have suffered many disappointments and setbacks, but she was always most charming. Underneath that charm, however, was a shrewd business woman.

She found that it was no good going against men all the time. Instead, she went with them and persuaded them gently to her way. In Miss Thurston's words: "She certainly knew how to do this, she could be so very persuasive."

Kenneth Wright sums her up: "A woman with a great gusto for life and an enjoyment of her profession. She believed in and worked for the place of women in professional life with high seriousness, but without militancy. There could have been no better advocate for the cause."[5]

A study of women Chartered Accountants in England, completed in 1977, disclosed that their demographics are very similar to those of women CPA's in the U.S.[6] Three-quarters of them were under thirty-five years of age—a direct result of the heavy influx during the past ten years. Over two-thirds are married, and among the married women, 53 percent had children. A surprising 44 percent of them had at least one child under five years of age.

There is a difference in the educational patterns of the English women Chartered Accountants as compared to those in the United States, a difference produced by the apprenticeship system used in England. Only 29 percent of the women Chartered Accountants in England had a university degree. However, formal education at the university level is required as a part of the articled clerkship, so that 59 percent, in addition to those with degrees, had some education at a level comparable to that given at universities in the U.S.

Another interesting statistic is the high percentage of women Chartered Accountants who are in public practice. The following comparative table shows that a higher proportion of women are in public practice than men.[7] The data suggest that a significant proportion of men leave public practice to take positions in industry and commerce, while the women move to another commitment within public accounting itself. The relatively high percentage of women in the "other" category is due to the fact that a larger proportion of them are not employed, having elected to devote their time to their families and children.

	Women	Men and women combined
In public practice	64%	48%
In industry and commerce	14%	37%
Finance and banking	1%	9%
Teaching	3%	1%
Other	18%	5%

As in the United States, women Chartered Accountants appear to be attracted to the area of income tax as a specialty. Over half of the women included in this study listed income tax as the area in which they claimed special expertise. One of the reasons for their concentration in this area is the fact that it allows more flexibility in their schedules and they do not have to be at the beck and call of their audit clients. However, it is also of interest that in England, as in the U.S., the taxation area has a shortage of qualified personnel. The existence of greater opportunities may be one of the reasons more women Chartered Accountants are moving in that direction.

Women around the world have the same set of problems when it comes to balancing career and family. English women Chartered Accountants are no exception. The study being cited here stated, "The heavy burden of responsibility led to tiredness, guilt feelings, resentment towards husbands who did not pull their weight and thankfulness to those who did, as well as recognition that a career similar to men was more difficult to pursue: "I feel I am at a disadvantage compared with most of my male colleagues in finding time. . . ."

IN CONCLUSION

The problems faced by women who have entered the accounting profession are similar in almost all of the countries in the industrialized free world. A study completed in England by the Institute of Personnel Management, Ashridge Management College, summarizes the problems and their antecedents very well. In that study a number of men and women professionals in England were interviewed in an effort to find out why women are discriminated against in their move up the career ladder. The study categorized the reasons into three basic groups—the existence of a rather rigid structure in many career paths, the attitudes of senior executives who decide promotions, and the attitudes of women themselves. These basic barriers are strikingly similar to those which are at work in the U.S.

Structure of Career Paths

The structure of career paths become established over time in almost all professions and organizations. The time-in-grade with one of the large public accounting firms is a classic example—three or four years to become a senior accountant, another three or four to manager, and a total of no less than ten for partnership. The numbers may differ from firm to firm, or from country to country, but the timing and the steps are relatively fixed. Of central importance—these times must be in strict sequence, with no break in between. In older organizations, such as the larger public accounting firms, these patterns were established before women came into the profession in significant numbers, and were patterned for men. There is no break permitted in this pattern. If a woman steps out of the pattern for six months or a year to begin a family, she will find reentry very difficult. Even with a formal arrangement with the firm's management concerning the maternity leave, the individual almost always sustains a loss in career development that far exceeds the time taken during the leave. The justification given for not permitting breaks in the career progression is that keeping up with developments in the profession is difficult even when employed; keeping up is virtually impossible when on leave. The rigid career path established for men does not provide for reentry points, nor does it even attempt to address the reentry problems which might exist.

The pattern of the career path in public accounting may be described as follows:

* A period of study and preparation, beginning in one's teens and culminating in one's early twenties. The commitment to the career must be made during this age bracket. In the United States this time is during the early years at the university, when majors and areas of concentration are selected; in England it is when the apprenticeship is arranged. Women, who typically commit themselves to long-term career decisions at a later age than men, find that the support system is geared for this early age bracket. Public accountants hesitate before hiring a new recruit who is past this traditional age. Although they do hire women approaching thirty, these women must have qualifications above the average person being recruited.

* After approximately three years of successful performance, there is a promotion to the lower supervisory grades. The public accountant must now be certified and must have settled into a specialty area within the profession—tax, auditing, or consulting. Specialties within each of these may also be necessary, such as auditing banks, or manufacturing, or governmental agencies. To have reached this stage is expected by the time one is in the mid-twenties. If not at this stage by the age of thirty, the individual is at a distinct disadvantage, regardless of how long he or she may have been with the firm.

* From this point on, geographic mobility is required, especially in multi-office firms. Balancing family commitments with career commitments now becomes more difficult for both men and women, but the societal view of men as the primary breadwinner places women at a disadvantage.

* By the early to mid-thirties, after ten years of experience, and having achieved a high degree of technical expertise in some area of the profession, the individual approaches a partnership position. The attitudes of those who make the partnership decision now assume paramount importance.

Attitudes of Senior Management

The attitude of senior management of public accounting firms can and will exert subtle but powerful influences on the career path of women. If subconscious biases exist, they will assign women to audits or to clients that are considered "suitable" for women. Financial activities, such as banks and insurance companies were the first to be deemed "suitable," along with non-profit activities such as governmental agencies, universities, school districts, and hospitals. There still exists strong resistance to assigning women to companies involved in heavy manufacturing, refining, and the production of basic metals. The type of assignment considered "acceptable" for women is frequently counterproductive to the woman's long-term development, for it may not be sufficiently main-stream to provide the technical specialty area necessary at the later stages of her career ladder. Further, good performance in one of these areas tends to be self-perpetuating, leading to additional assignments in that same area. Thus the woman may be left in that area and may not be adequately developed for the wider management responsibilities which are considered necessary at the partner level.

Women's Attitudes

Some studies have found that women, in general, tend to have less confidence in their ability to tackle a job. When asked about their strengths and weaknesses, women tended more than men to start by describing their weaknesses and did not emphasize their strengths quite as much as did men. This has important implications, in public accounting especially, for it could reinforce in men the attitude that women are not sufficiently forceful to stand up to clients in a toe-to-toe disagreement about audit standards or the application of accounting principles.

Women tend, according to these studies, to assume more than men that competence in their work and their technical ability will move them up the career ladder. Thus there is reliance on the supposition that they will be noticed by superiors and be rewarded for good performance at their current levels. There is less overt action on the part of women, again according to these studies, to create whatever conditions must exist for the next step up the ladder. This does not mean that women are less ambitious or less willing to sacrifice, but it does imply that they are less likely to actively work at *creating* the conditions which lead to promotion. This supposition implies that without backstabbing or resorting to belittling others, one can actively work toward creating the conditions in which a step up the ladder is possible. According to these studies, men tend to work more actively at creating such possibilities than do women.

That the technical qualifications of women in the profession are equal to those of men is rarely questioned today anywhere in the world. The performance of women on the professional examination is evidence of this, and awards to women are received around the world for their scores on the examination. At a time when the membership of The Institute of Chartered Accountants of Scotland was composed of 3 percent women and 97 percent men, women won the Gold Medal for highest score in two out of five years.[8] Similarly, awards began to be earned by women in Canada as soon as they began taking the exams in any appreciable number. A first place score was earned by Pamela Jermey of Toronto in 1976; two years later in 1978, top national honors went to Peggy Bennett of Mississauga, Ontario.[9] Similar experiences could be recited for other countries, for the entrance of women into the profession in any country will quickly be followed by their making top scores on the certifying examination.

In general, women have been accepted into the accounting profession in all the industrialized free countries. Their technical and psychological qualifications are apparent, while there are few remaining questions concerning their ability to perform the demanding tasks required for success in the profession. The one last remaining barrier in most countries of the world appears to be the resistance of the established male power structures within the profession, and this barrier is beginning to crumble. The decade between 1975 and 1985 has produced profound changes within the profession. Perhaps by 1995 there will be no significant barriers remaining.

REFERENCES

1. Institute of Personnel Management, *Employee Potential: Issues in the Development of Women,* London, 1980, p. 11.
2. Stockman, E., "Women Accountants in Other Countries," *The Woman CPA,* Vol. 33, No. 4, July, 1971, pp. 5–13.
3. Silverstone, R. and Williams, A., "Recruitment, Training, Employment and Careers of Women Chartered Accountants in England and Wales," *Accounting and Business Research,* Vol. 9, No. 34, Spring, 1979, pp. 105–121. Copyright © 1979.
4. Silverstone, R. and Williams A., op. cit., p. 106.
5. Robinson, J., "Ethel Watts—The Spirit of a Pioneer," *Accountancy,* Vol. 85, No. 973, September, 1974, pp. 54–55.
6. Silverstone, R. and Williams, A., op. cit., pp. 109–110.
7. Silverstone, R. and Williams, A. op. cit., p. 111.
8. Dunlop, A. B. G., "Women Accountants," *The Accountant's Magazine,* Vol. 78, No. 814, April, 1974, pp. 117–118.
9. "Ladies First—Again," *CA Magazine,* Vol. 112, No. 2, February, 1974, p. 22. See also "First Lady," *CA Magazine,* Vol. 110, No. 1, January, 1977, p. 9.